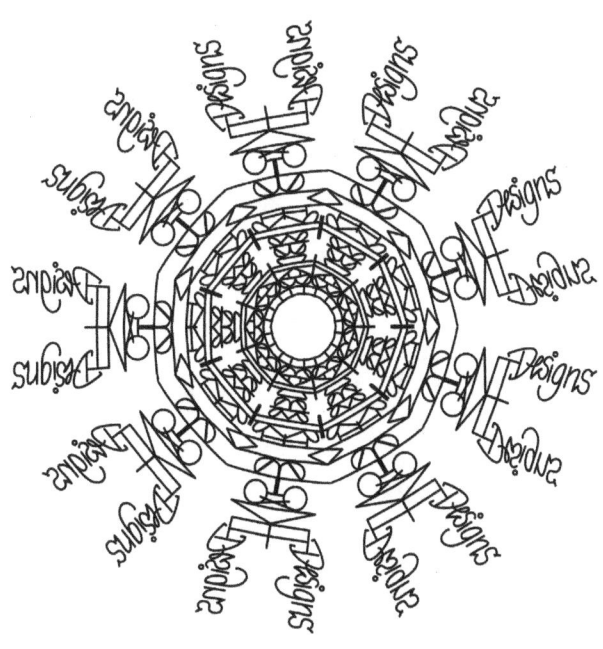

Mandala Designs Created by Artist
Heather Trimeloni

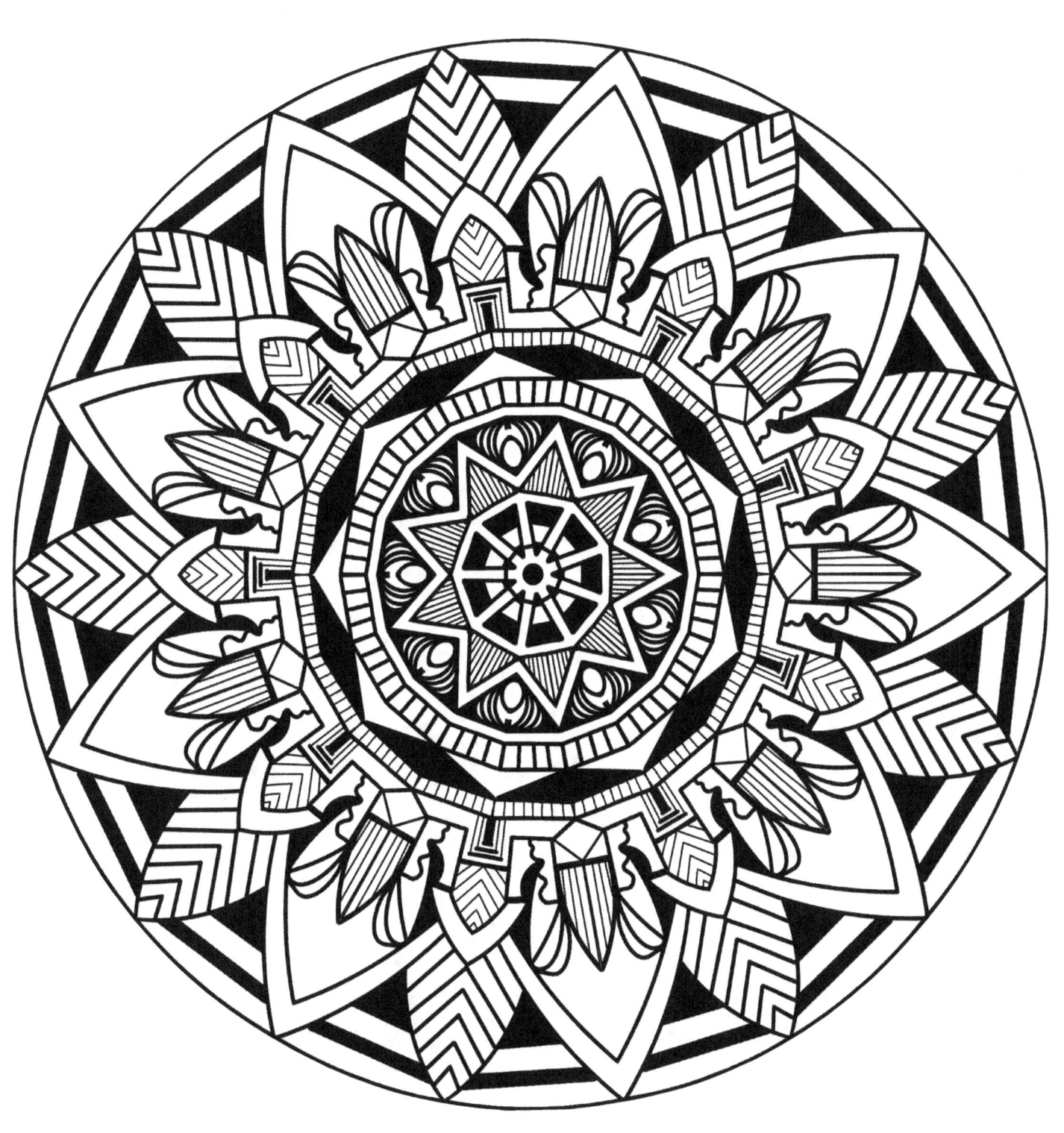

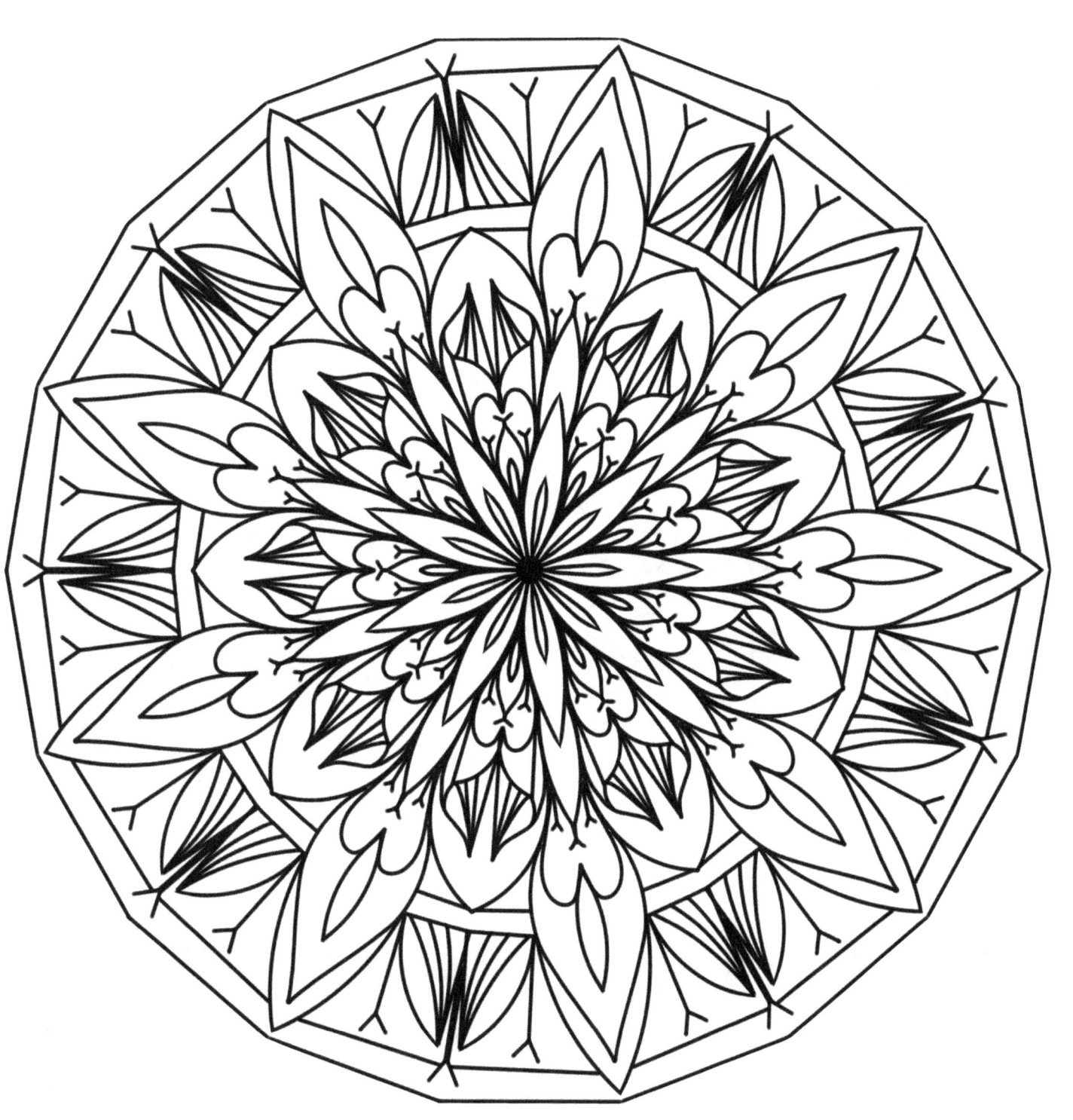

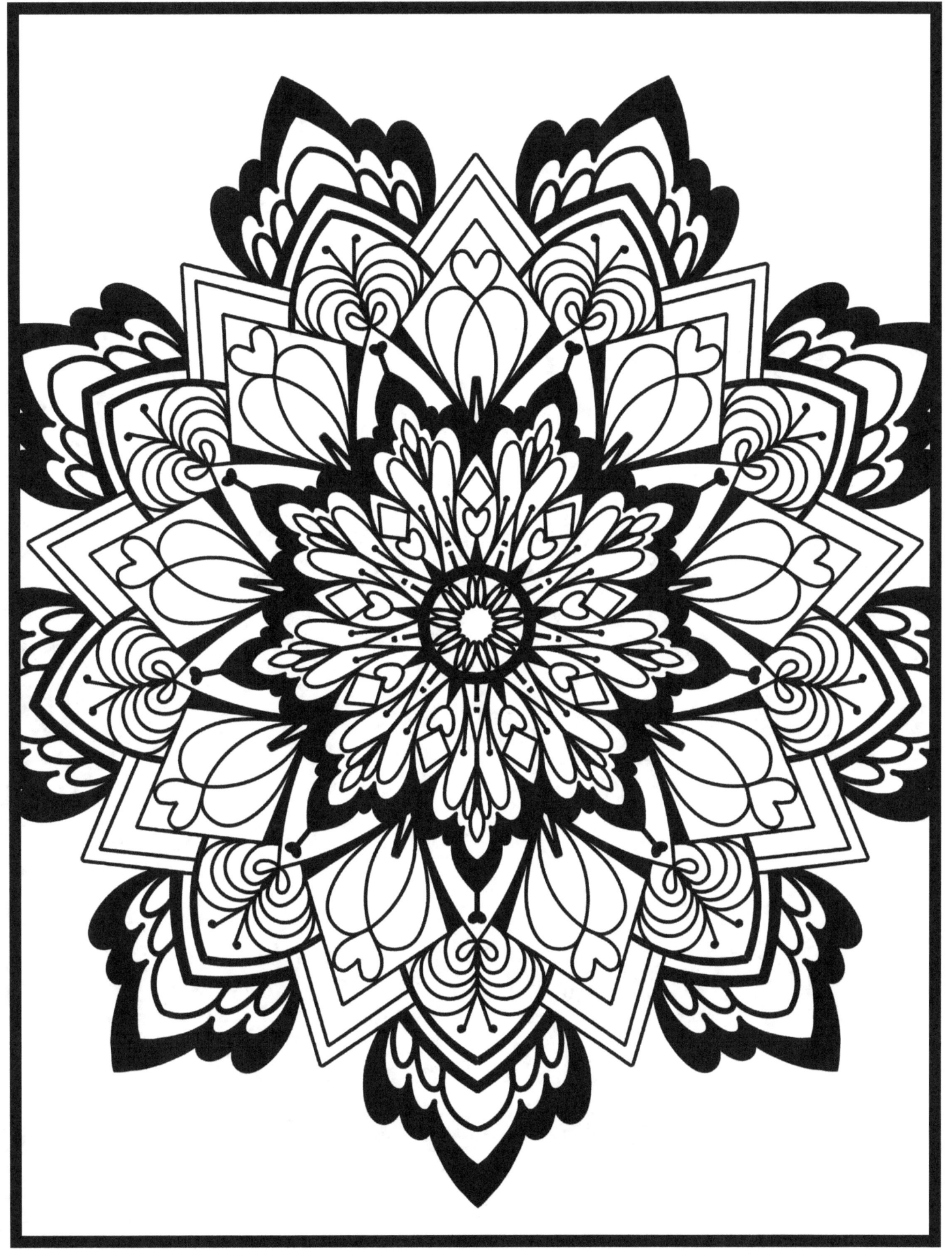

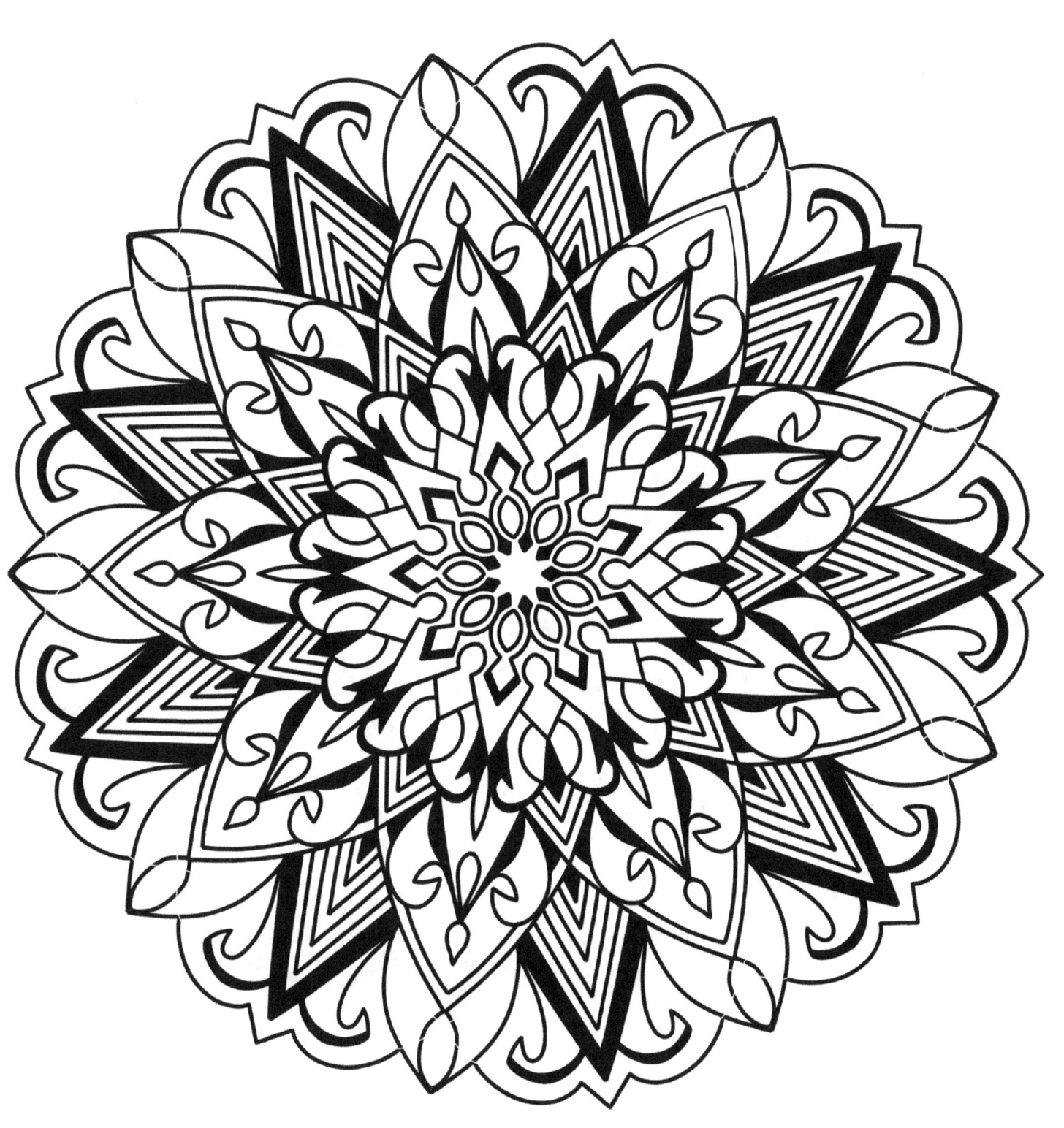

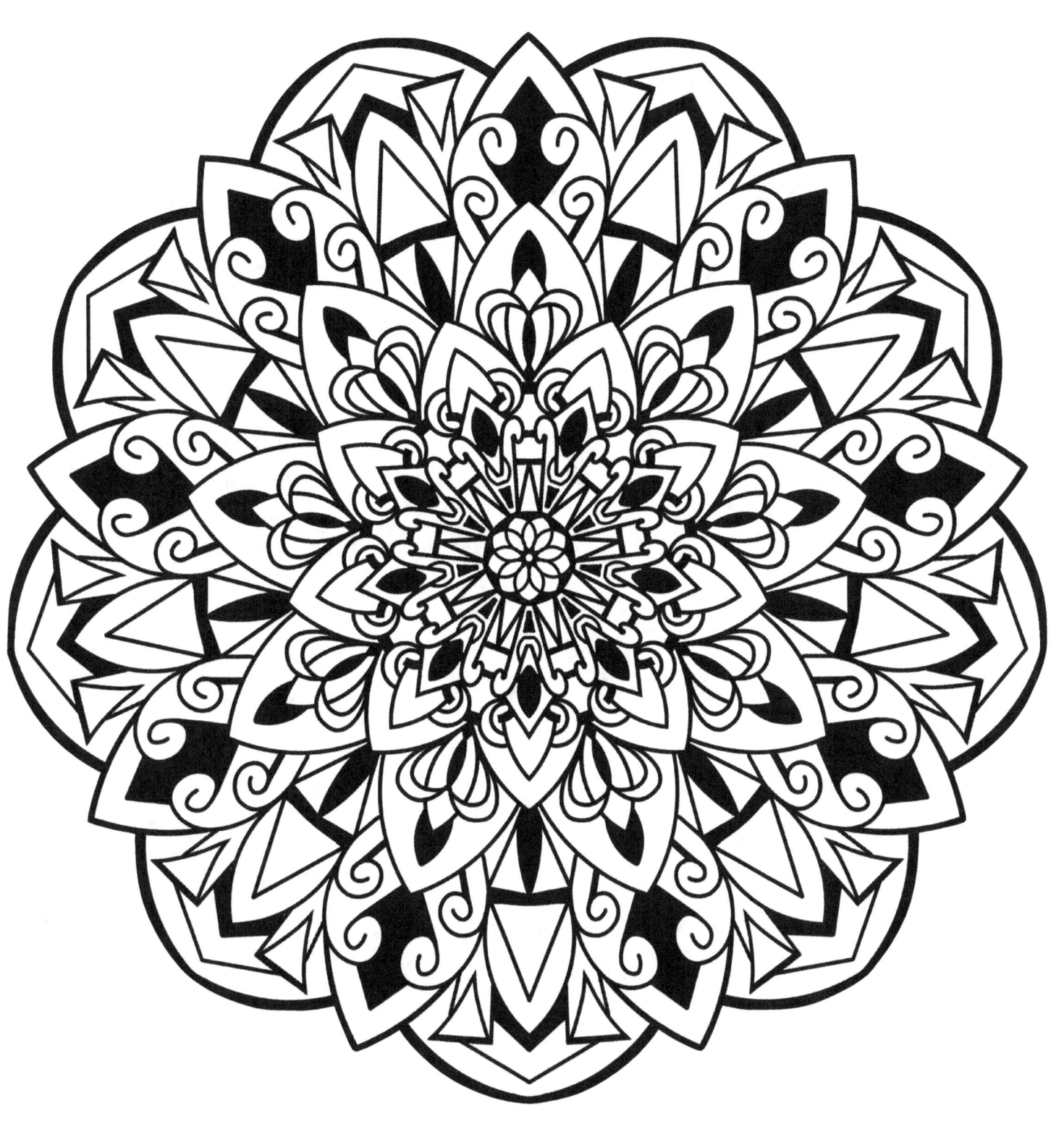

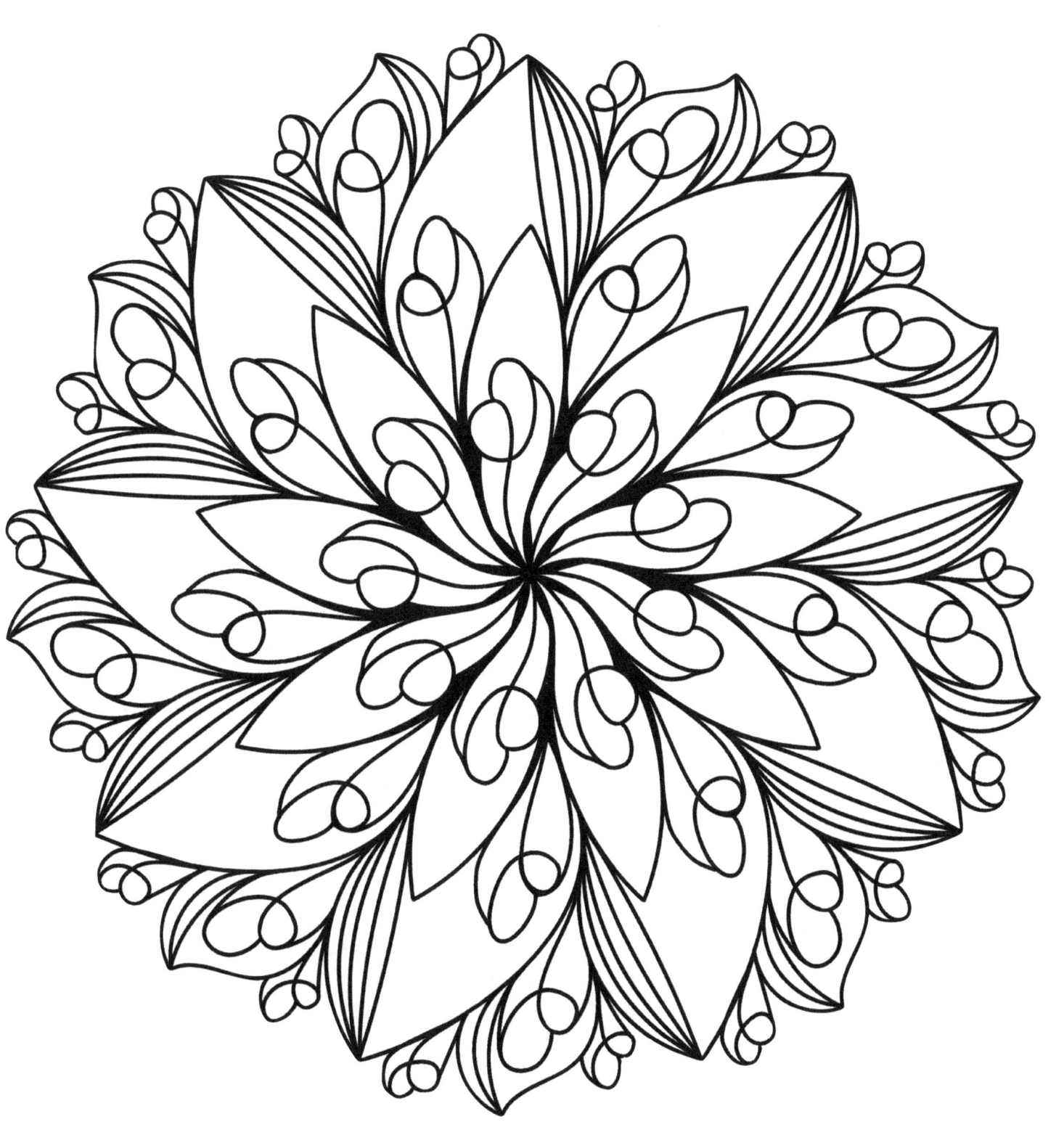

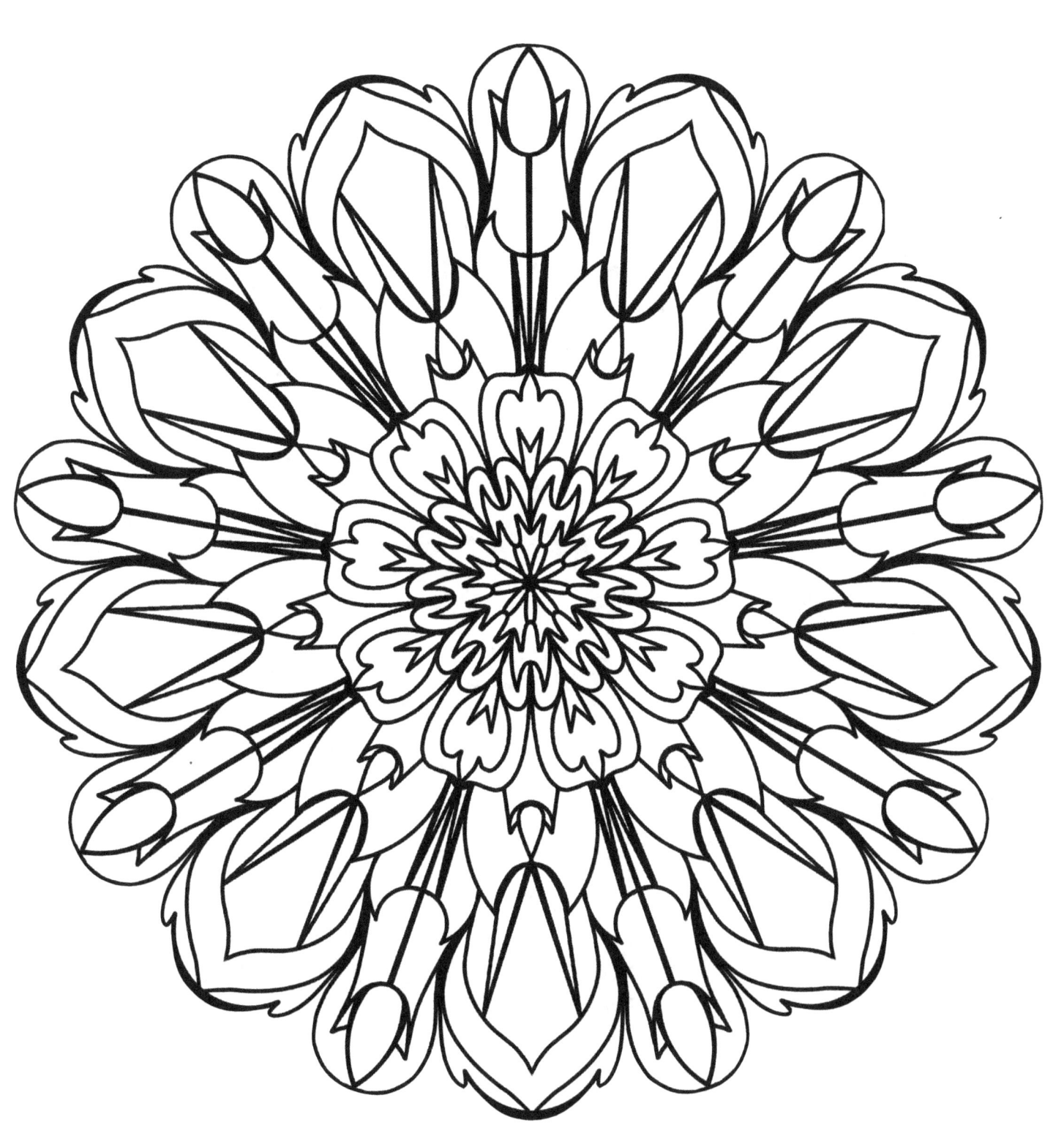

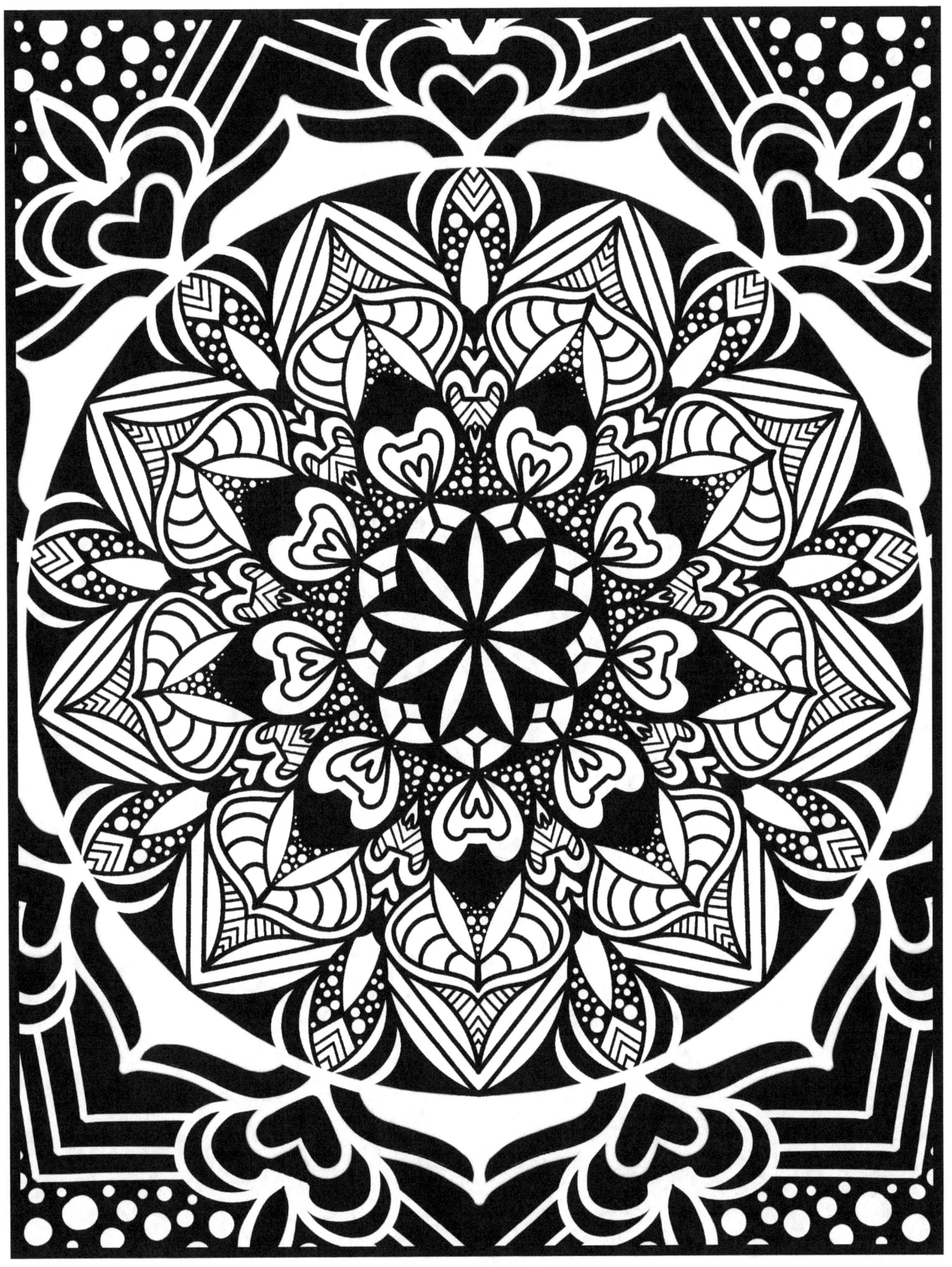

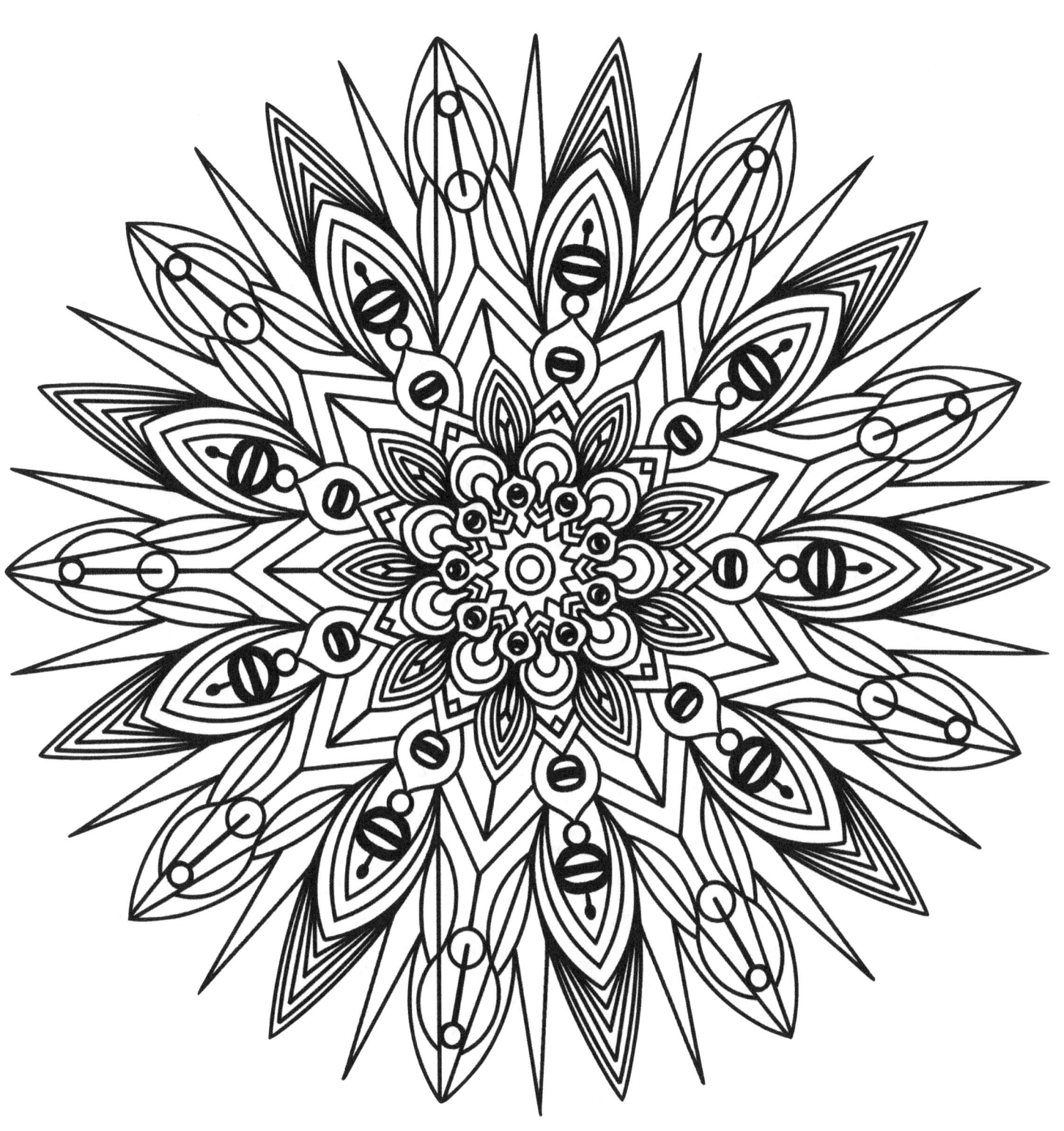

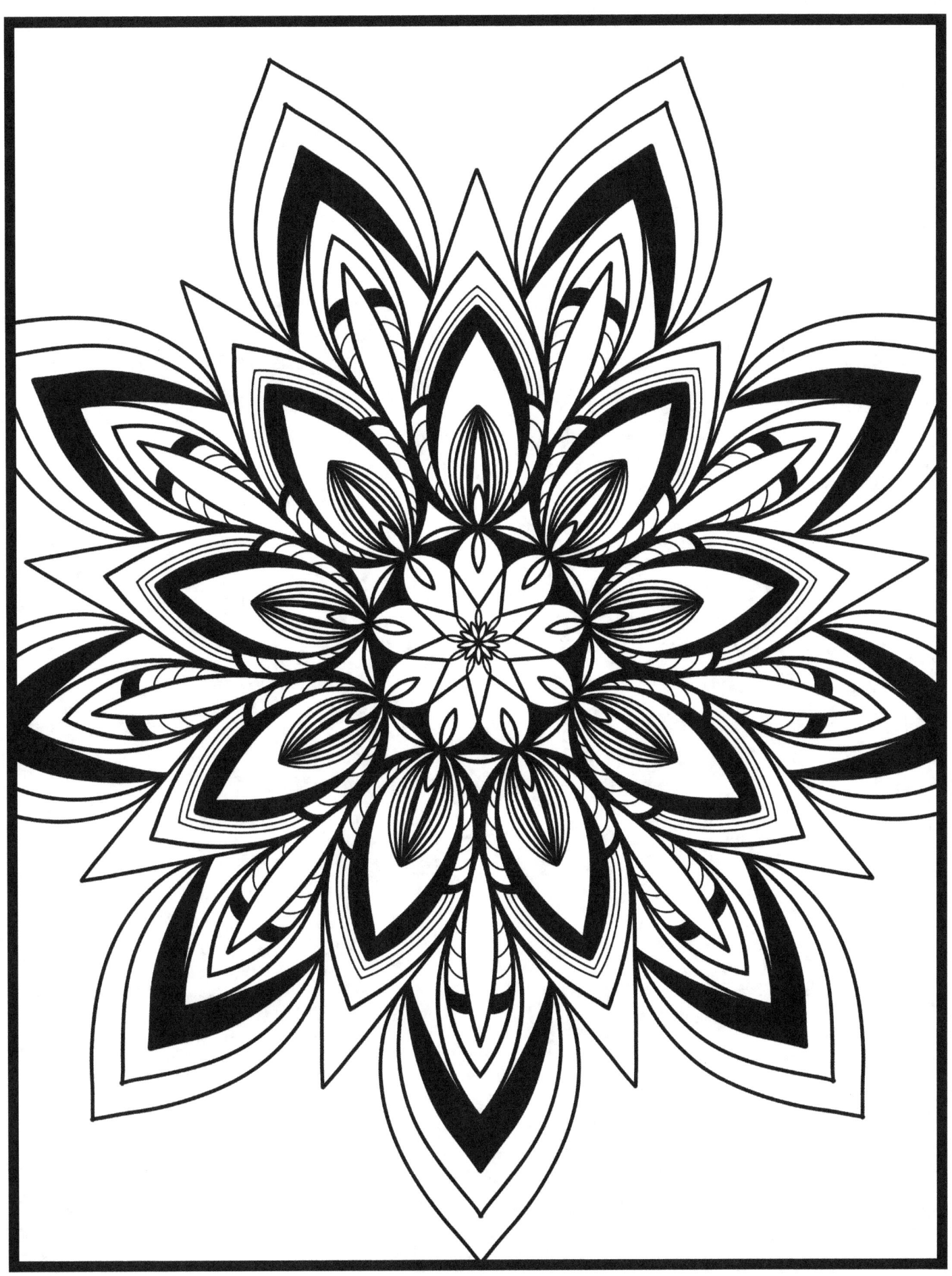

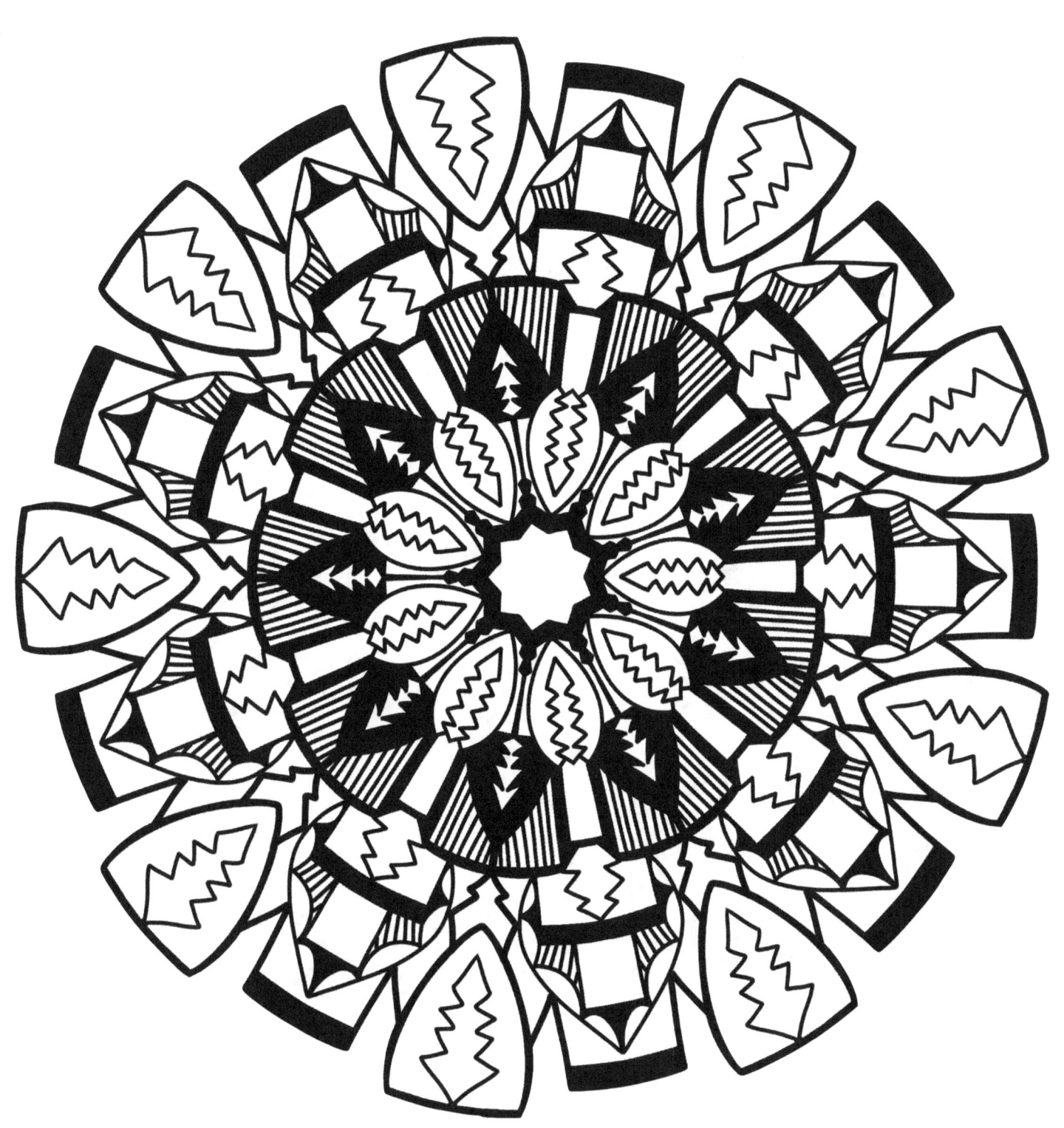

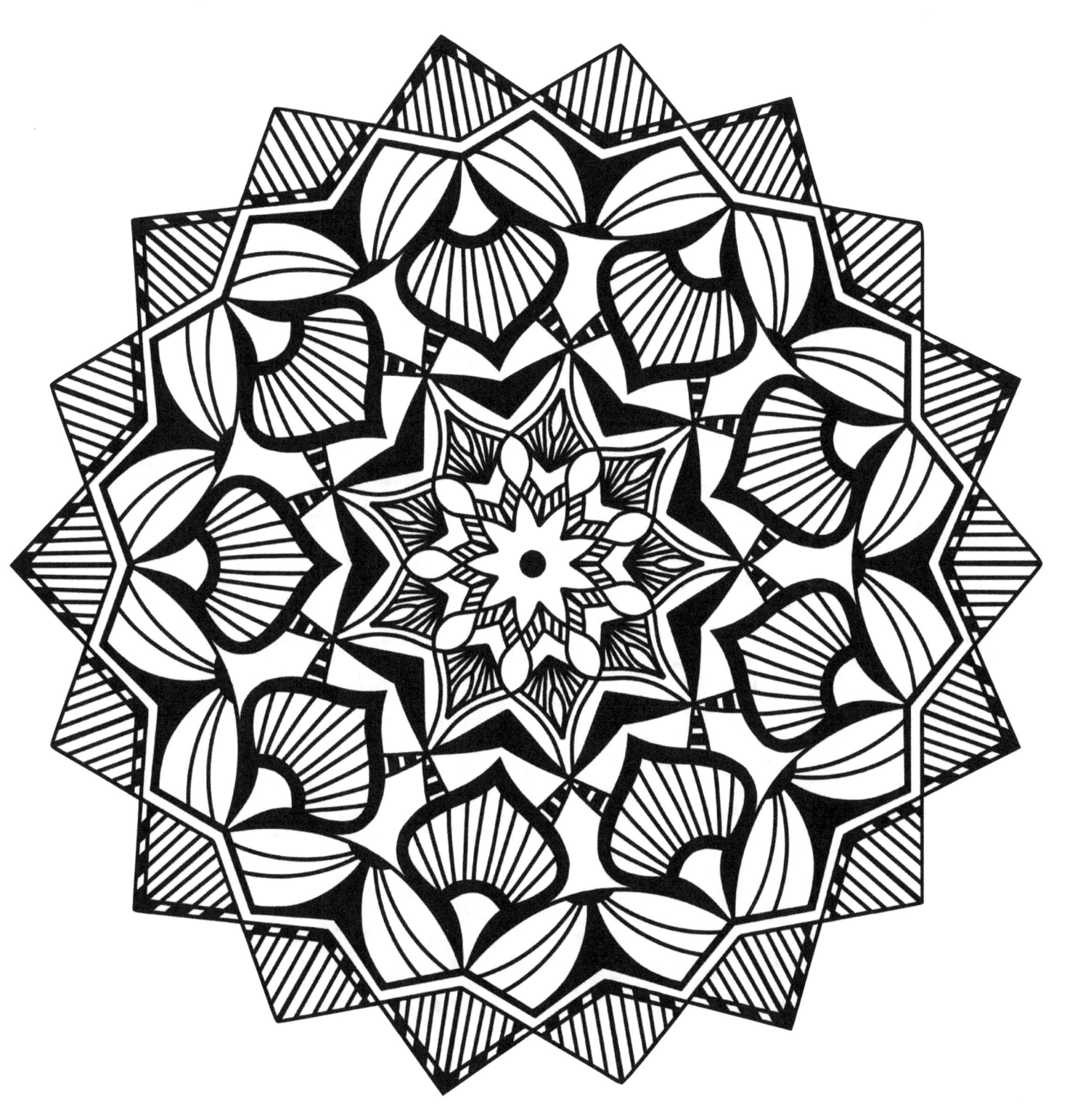

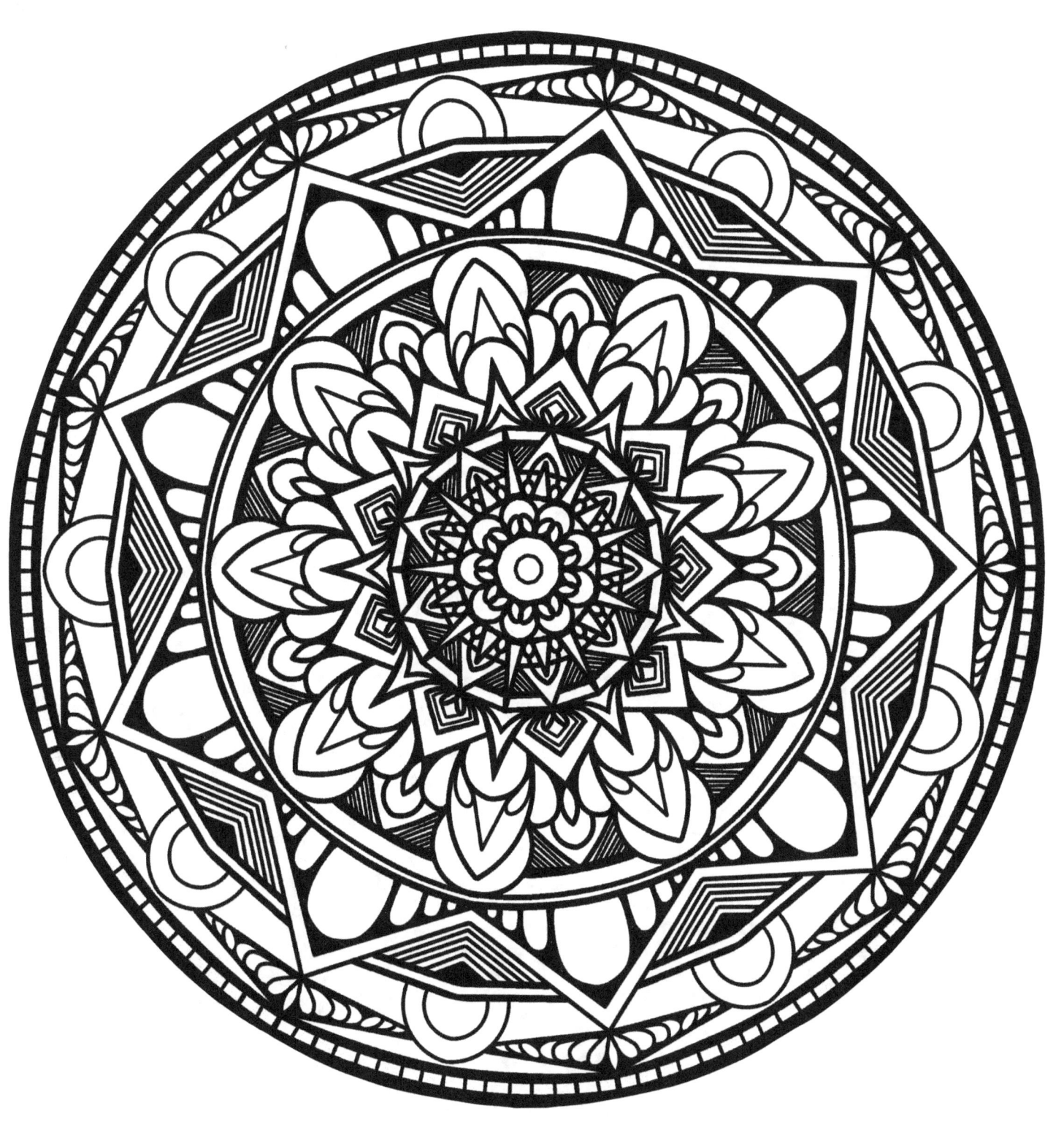

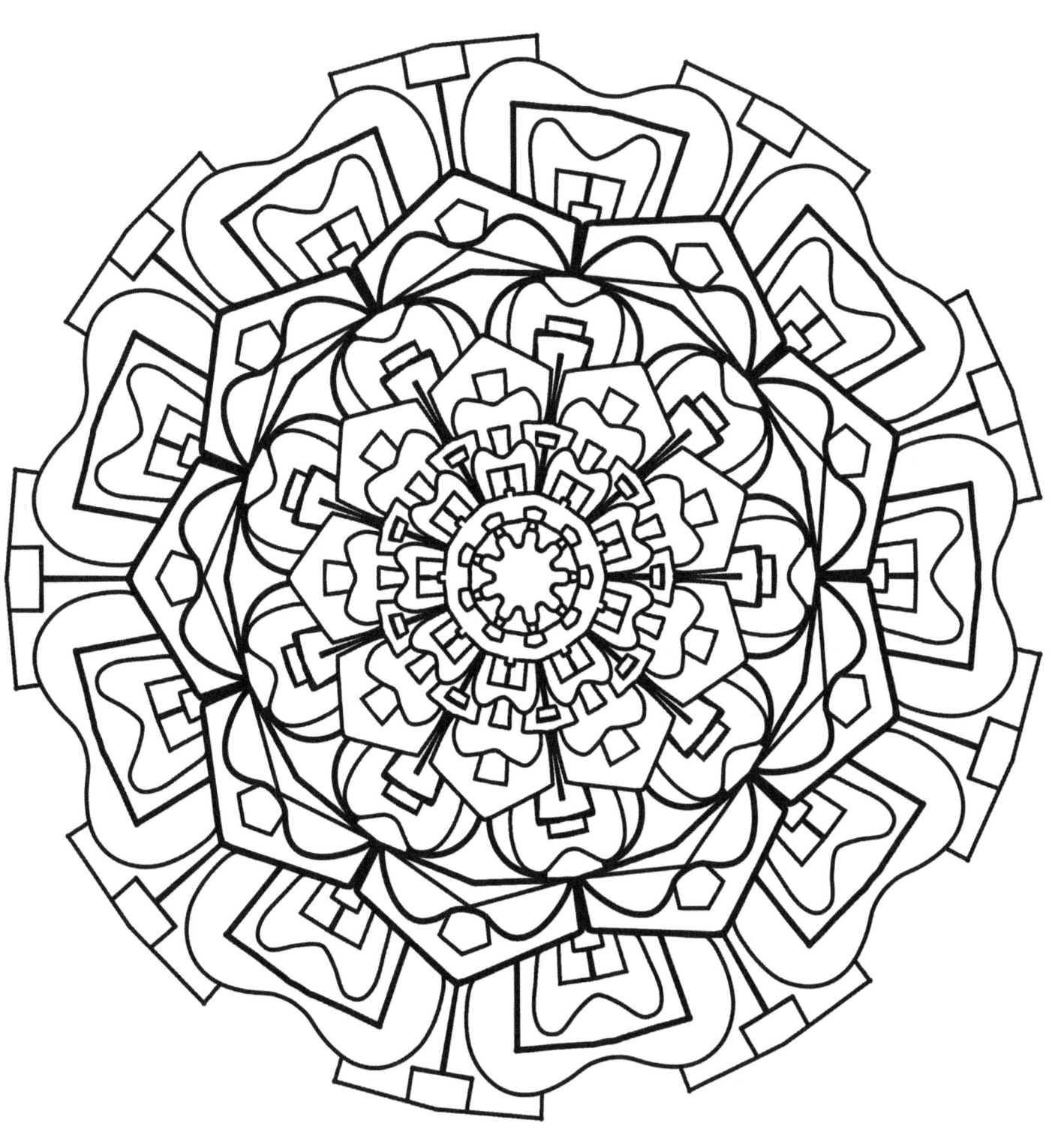

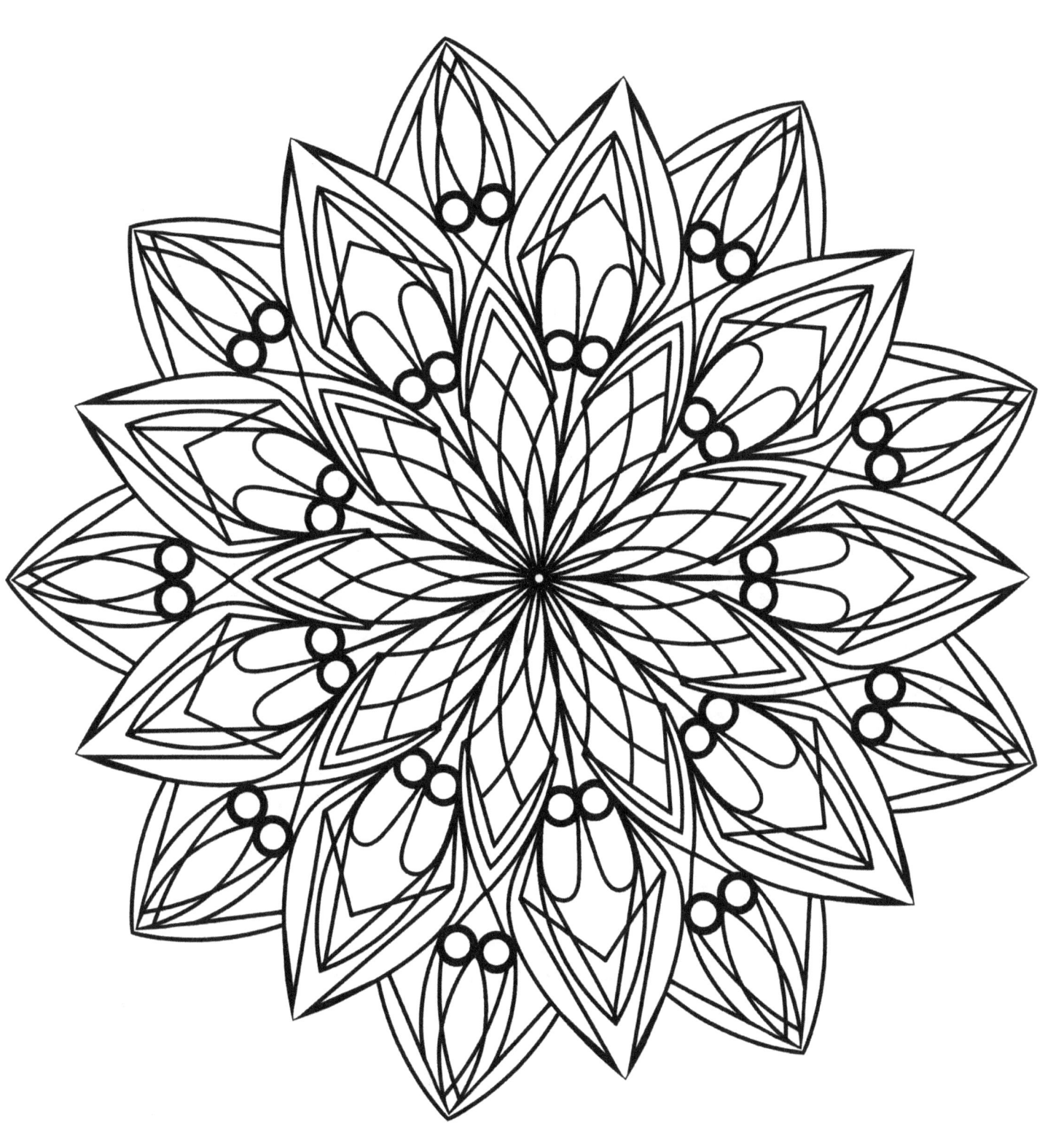

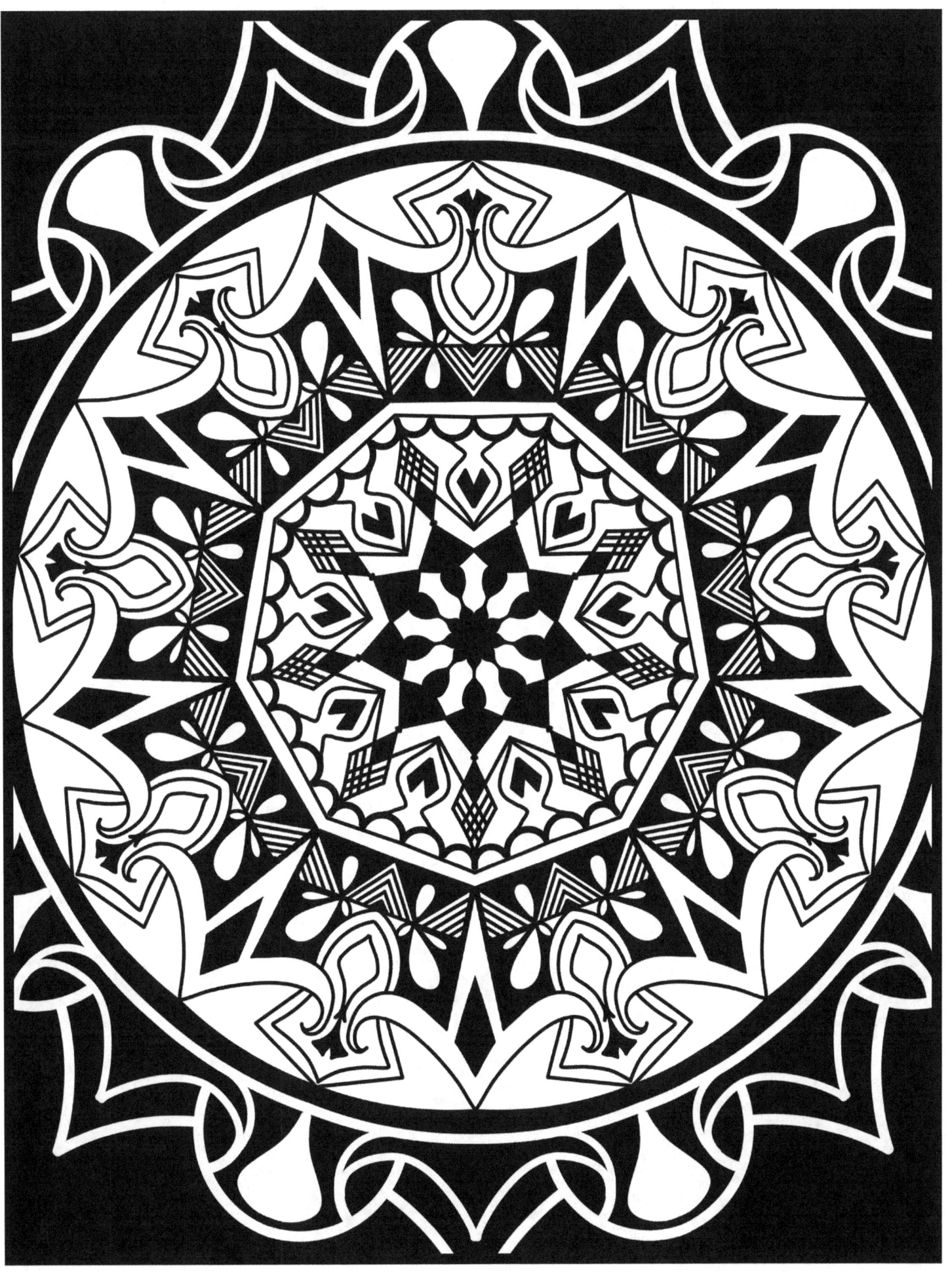

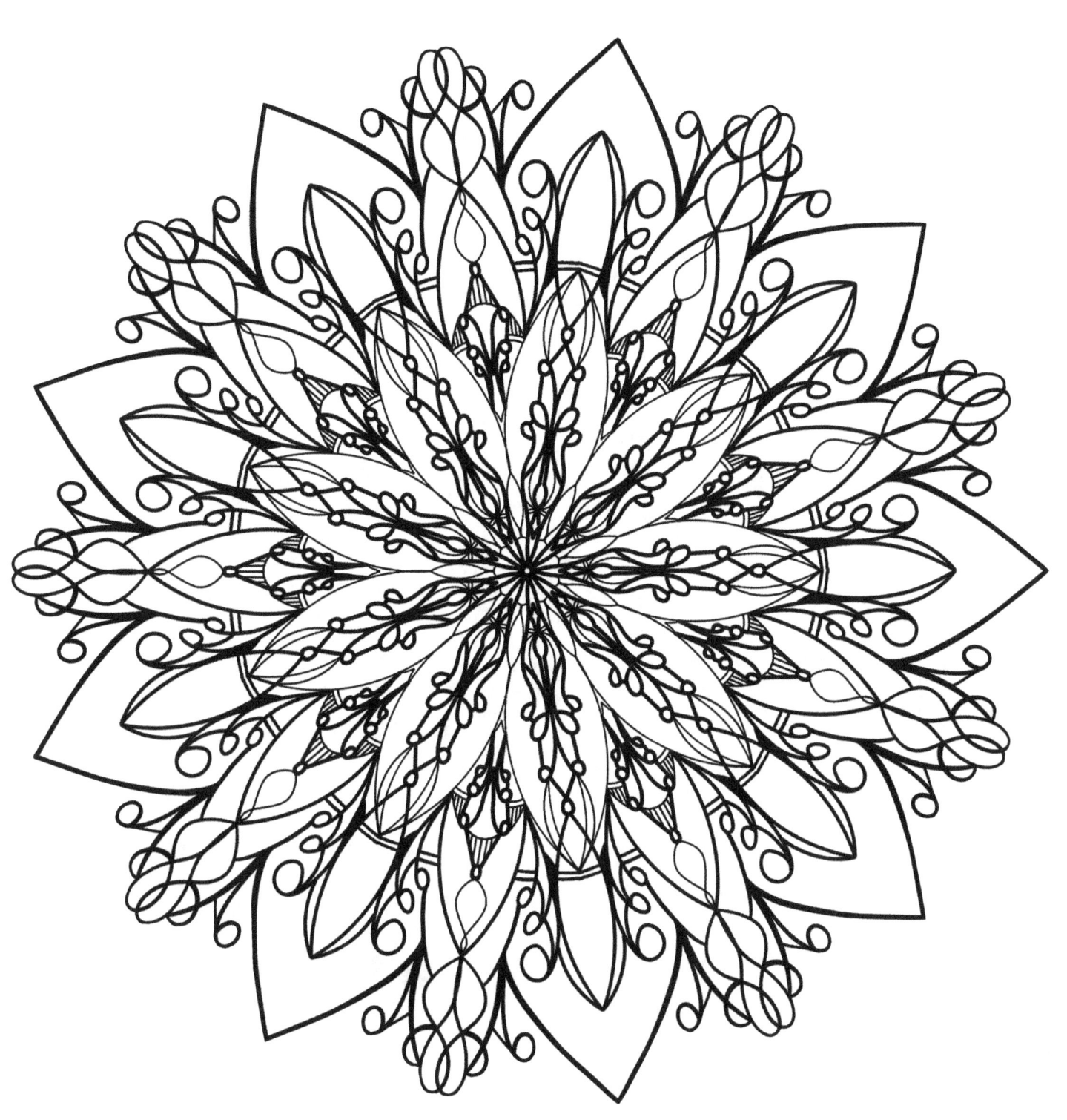

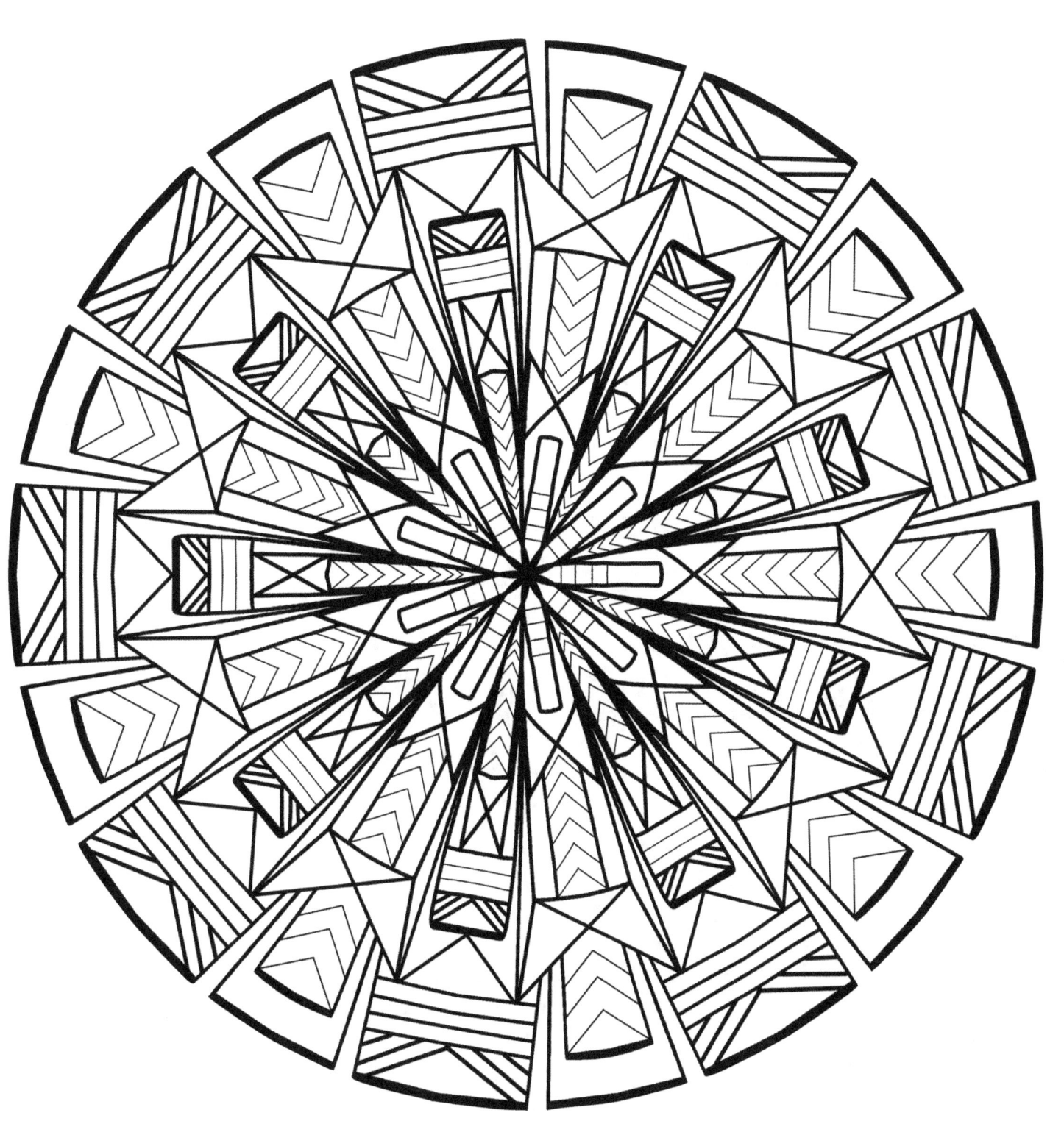

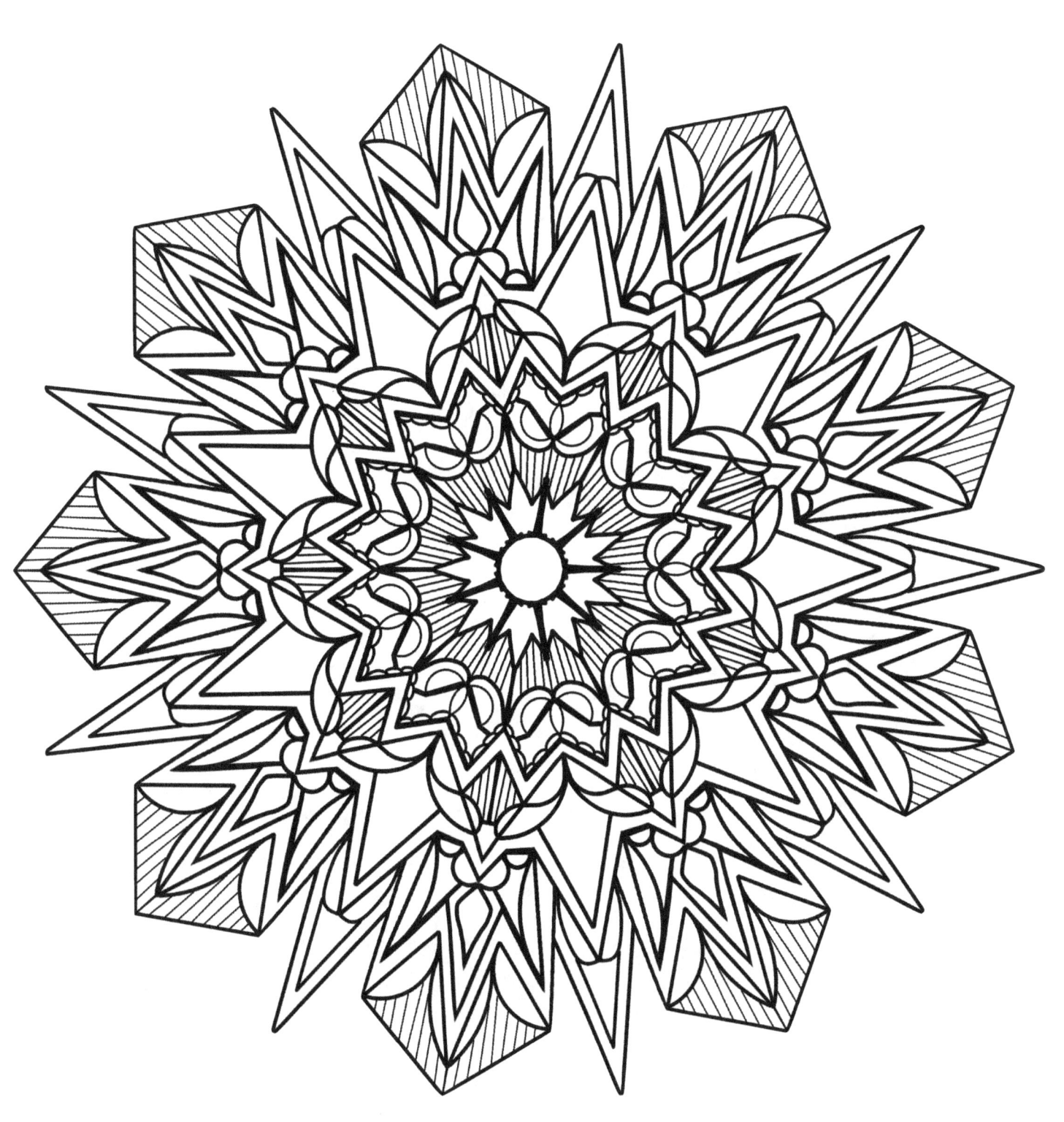

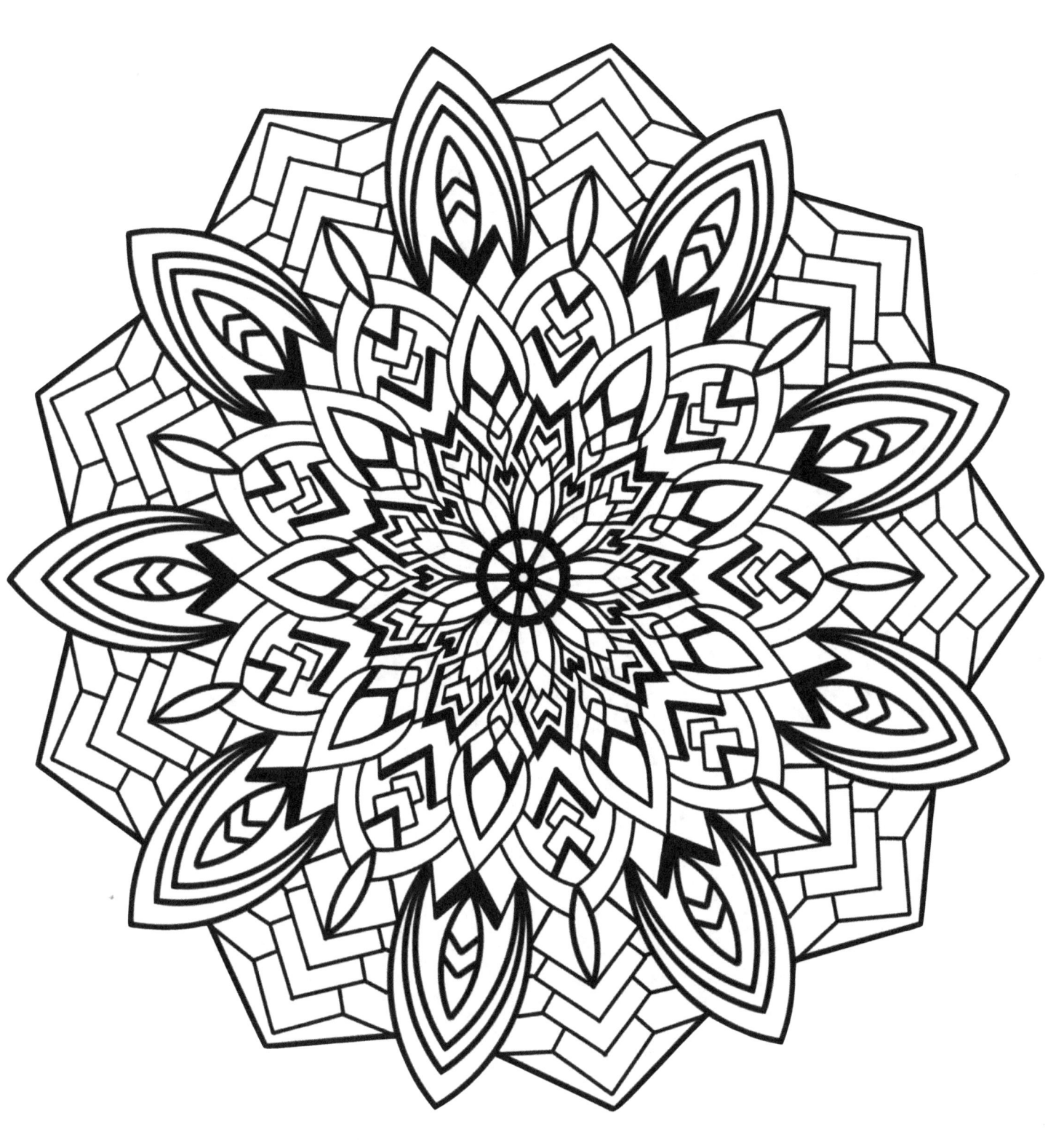

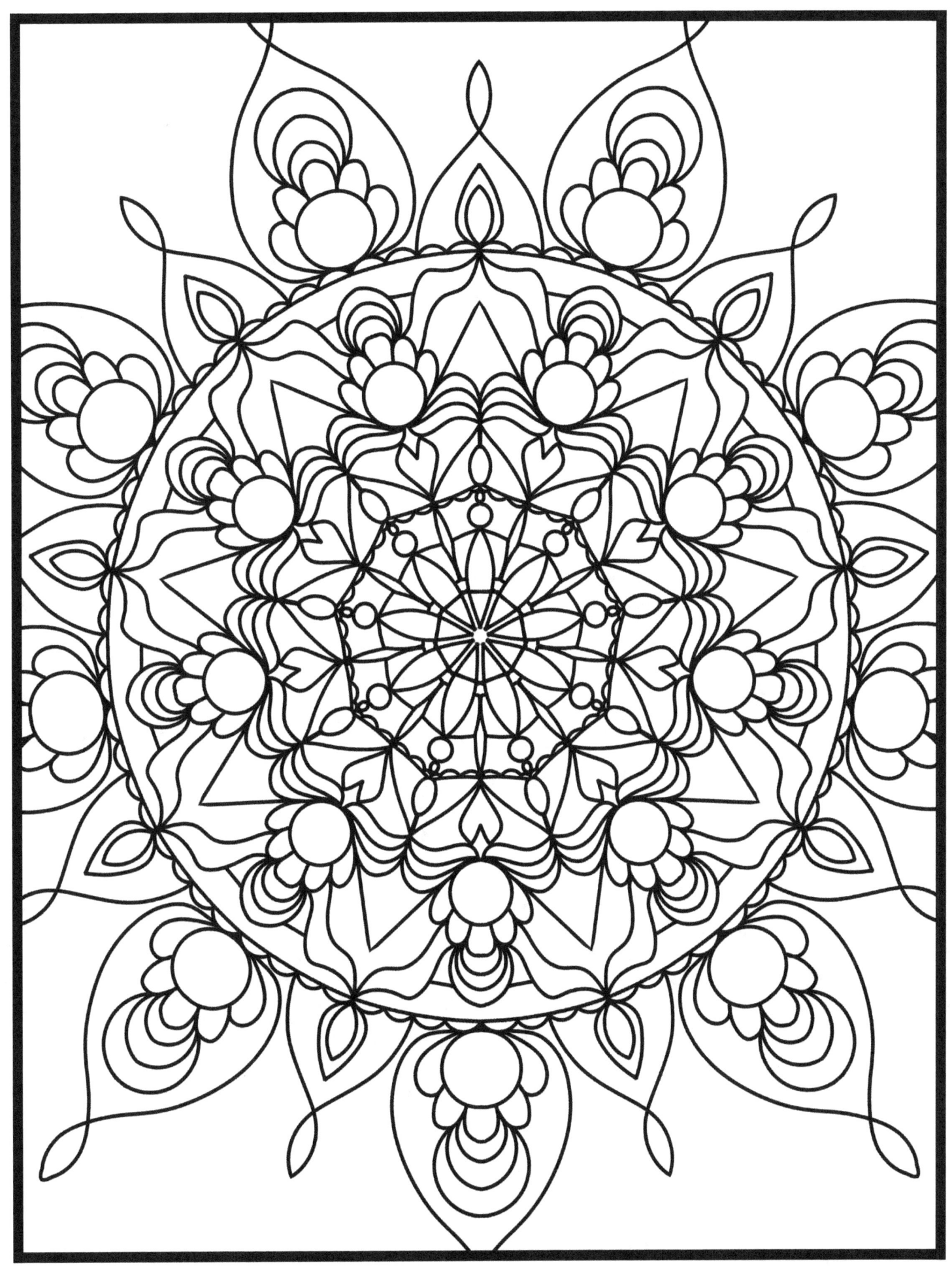

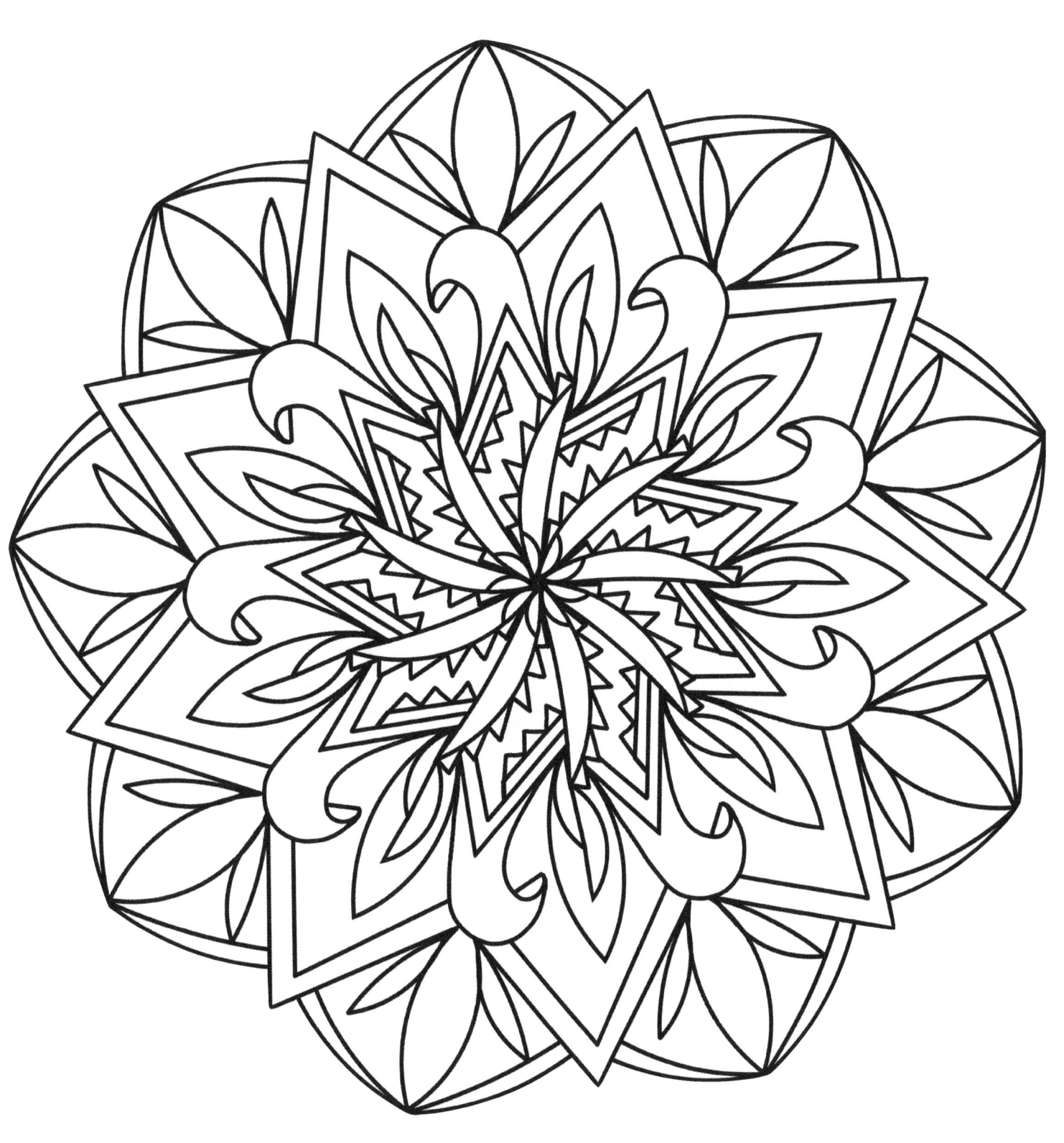

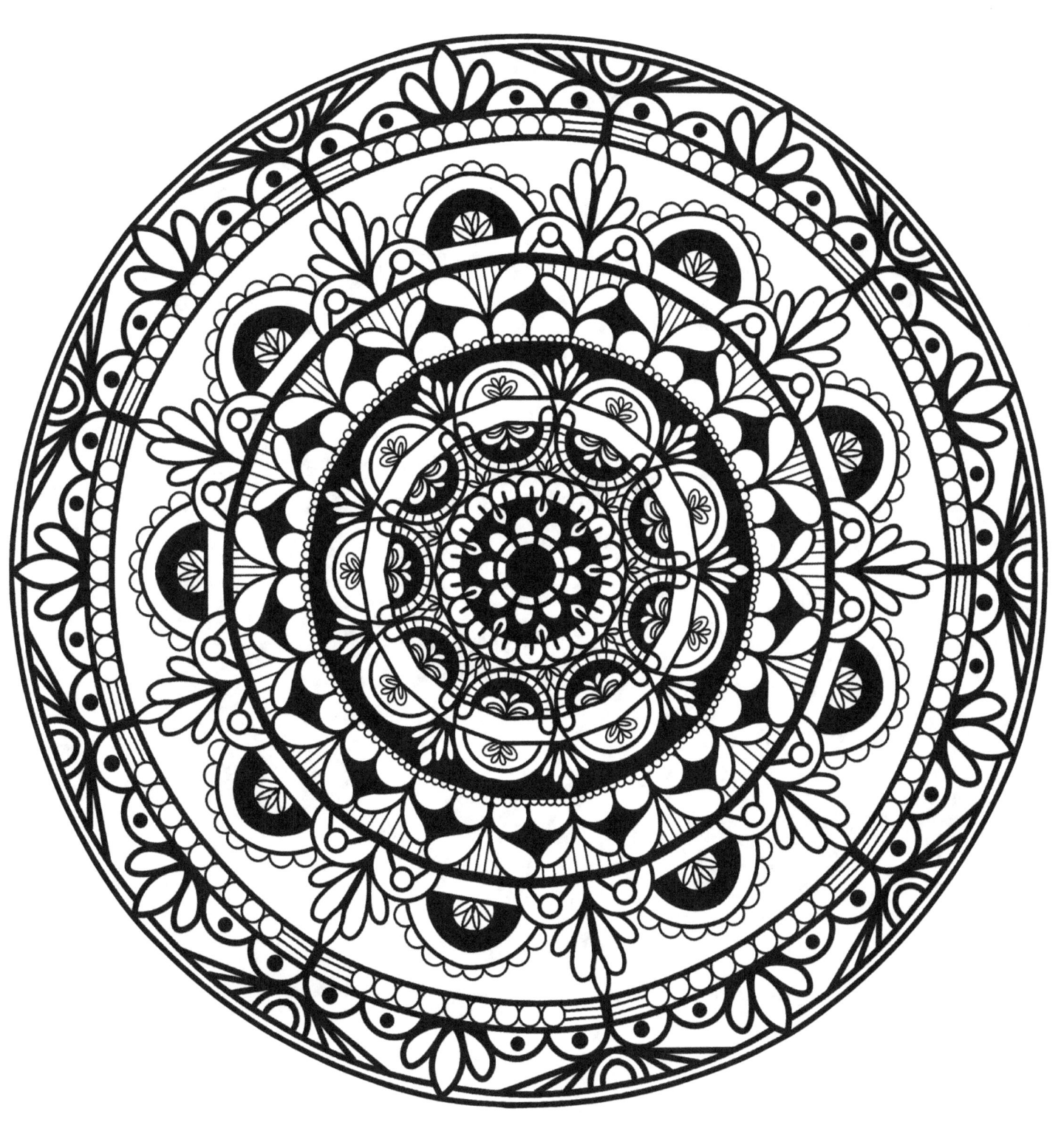

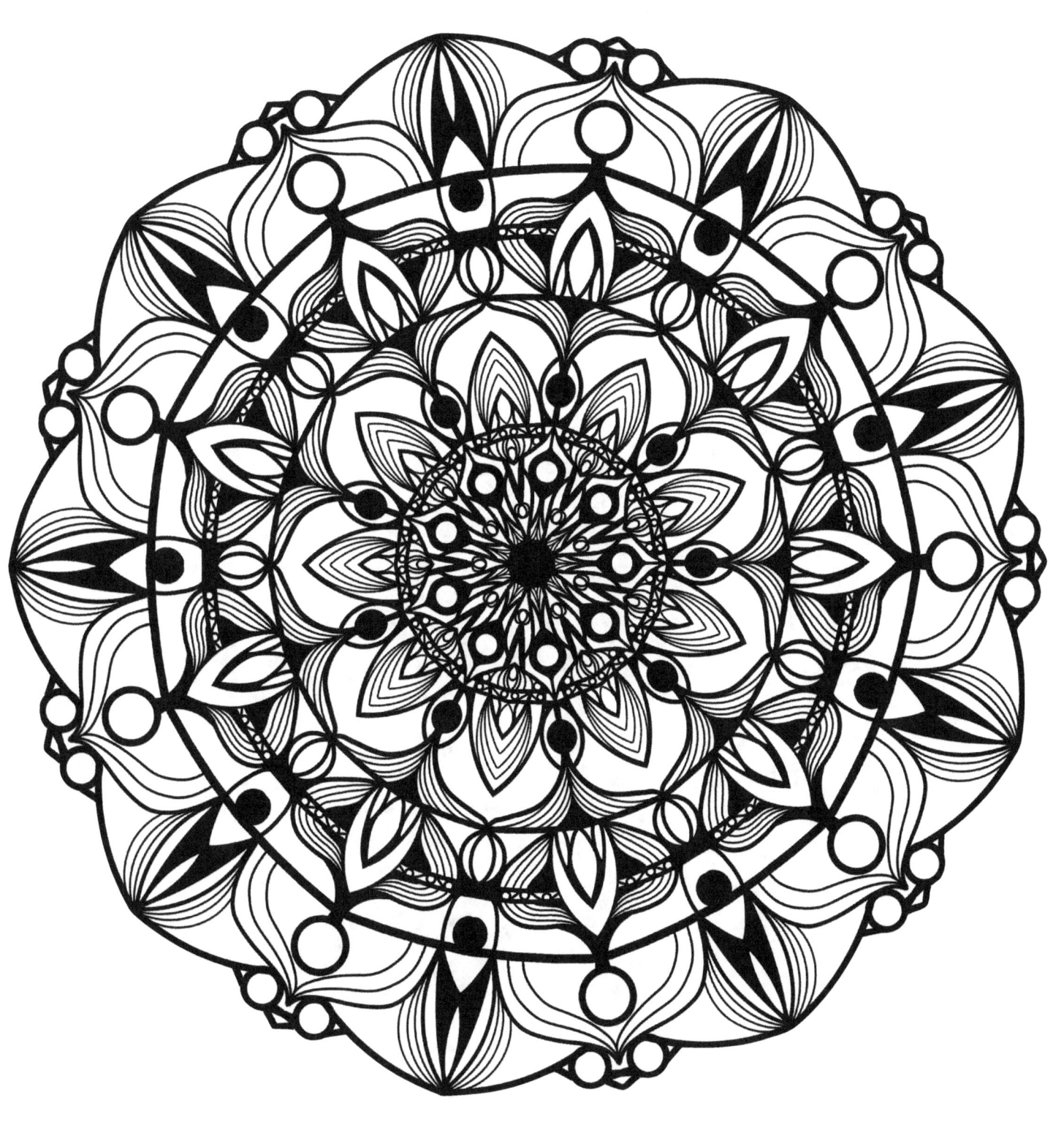

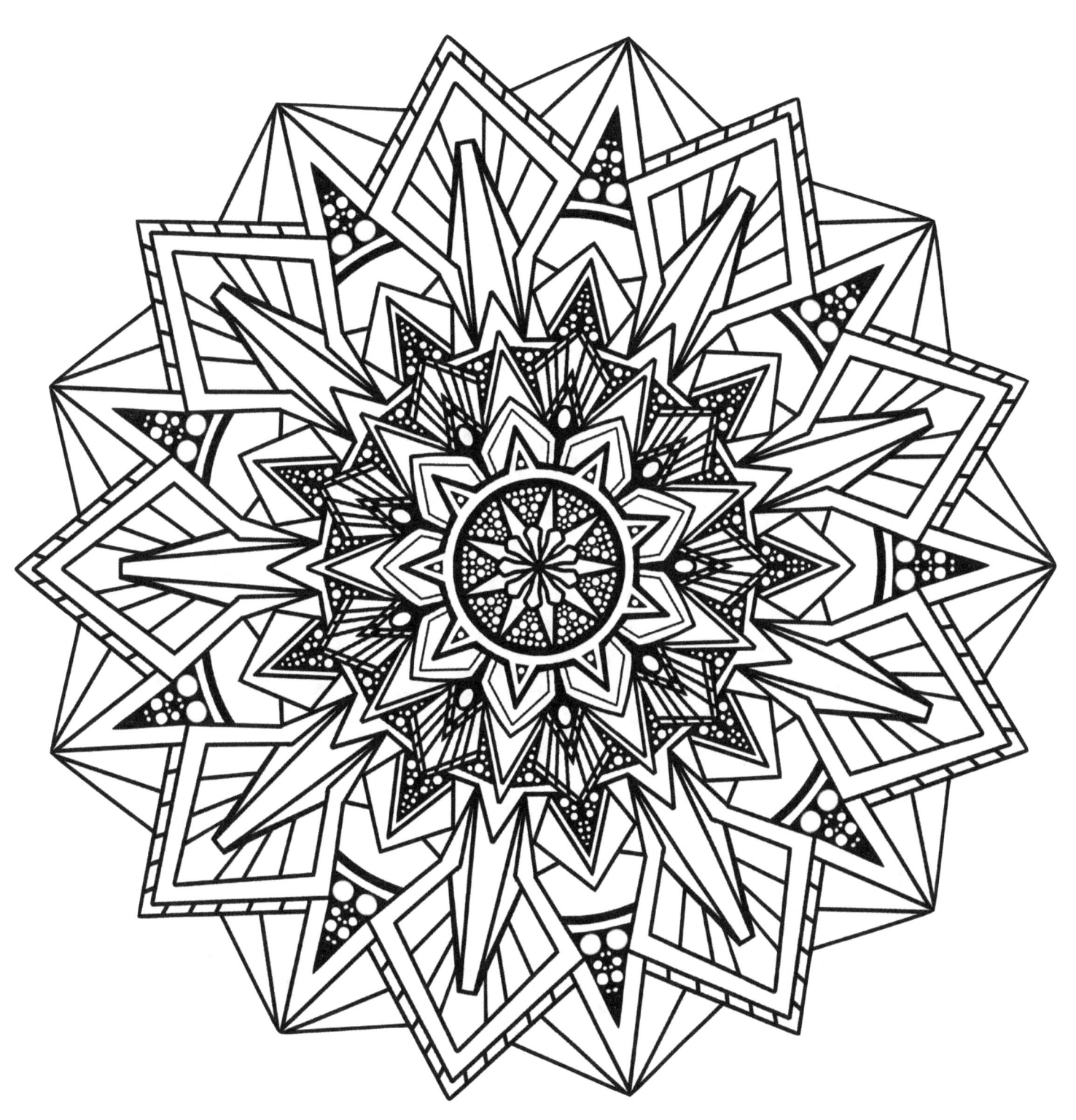

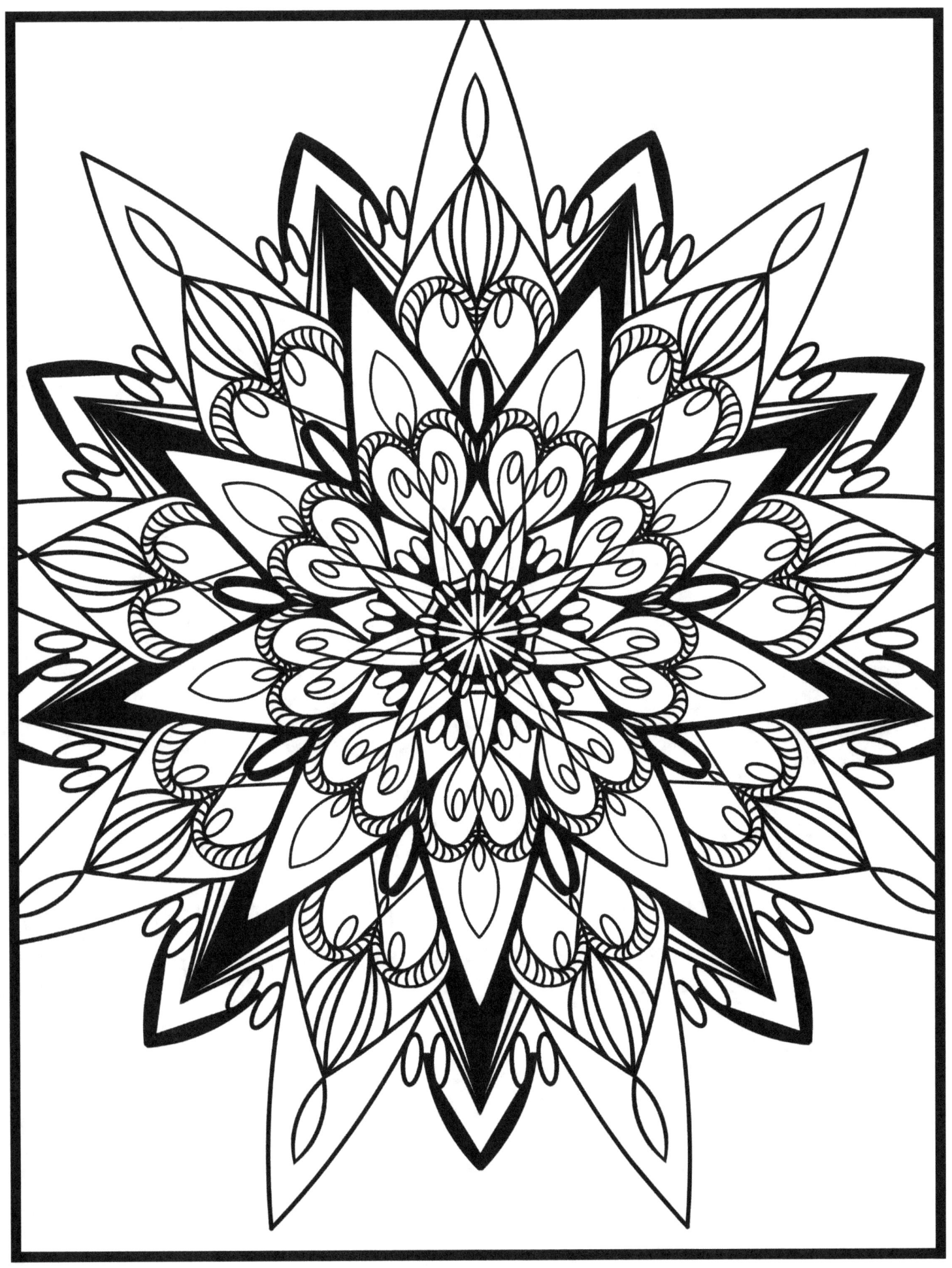

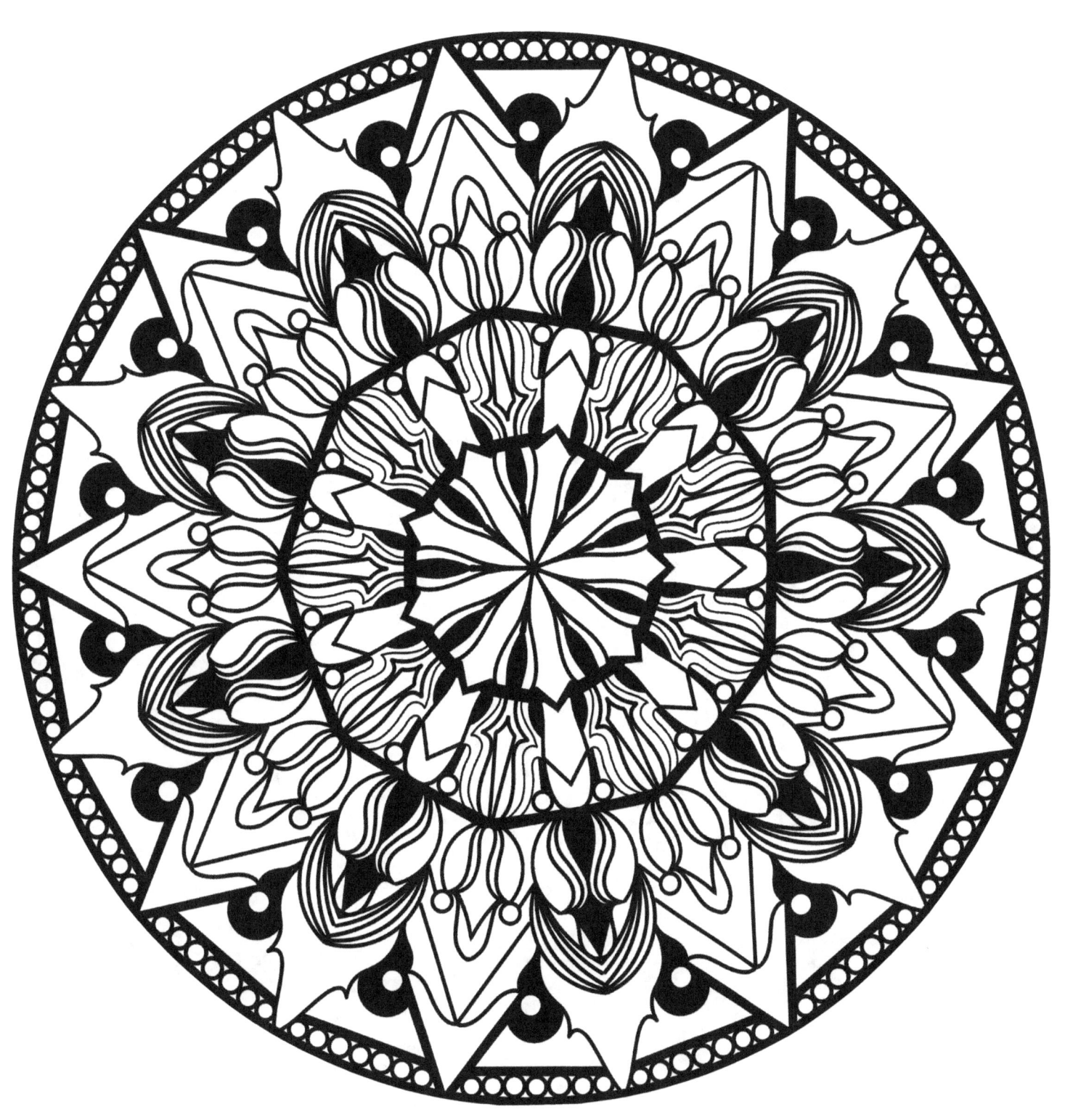

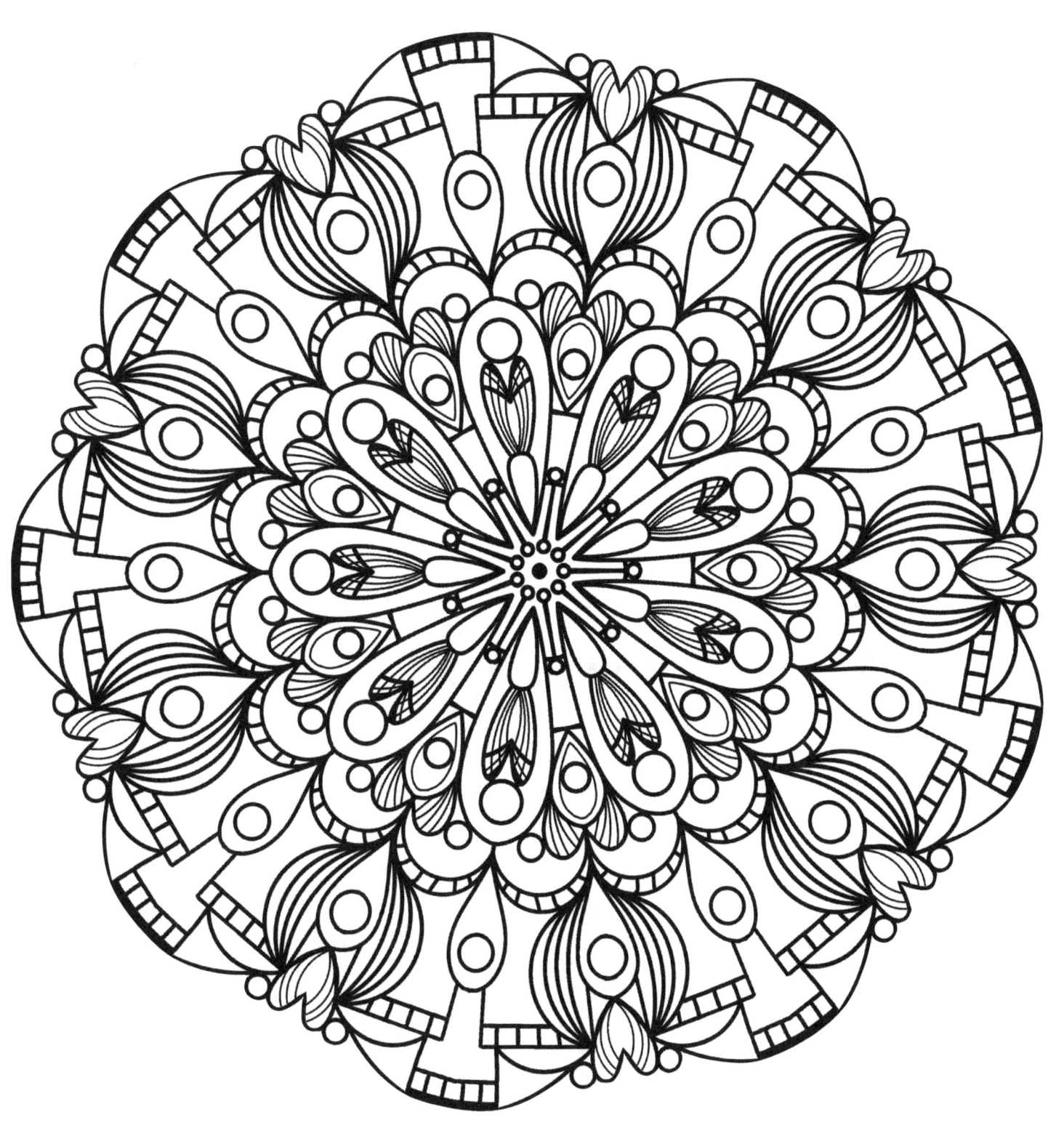

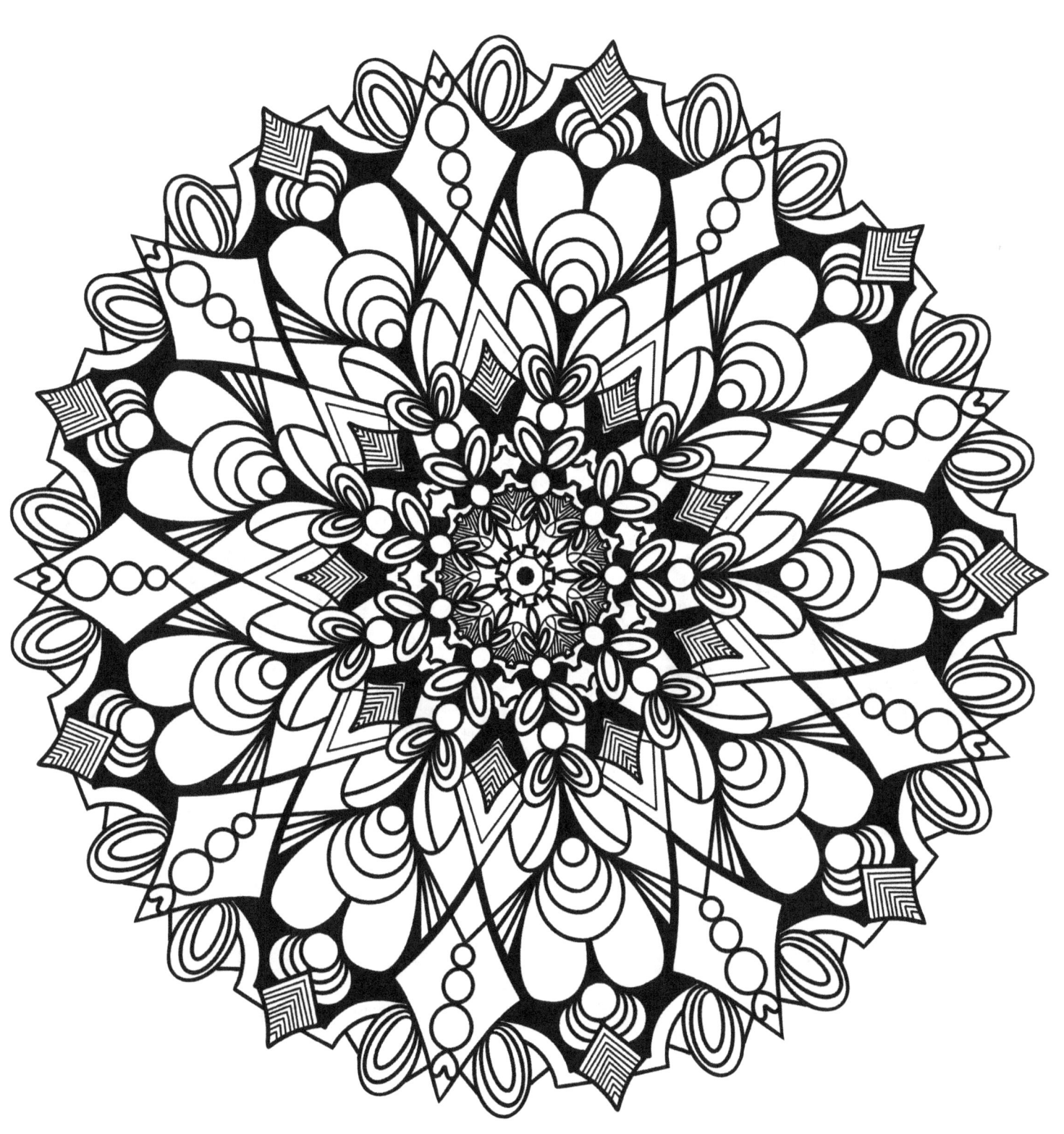

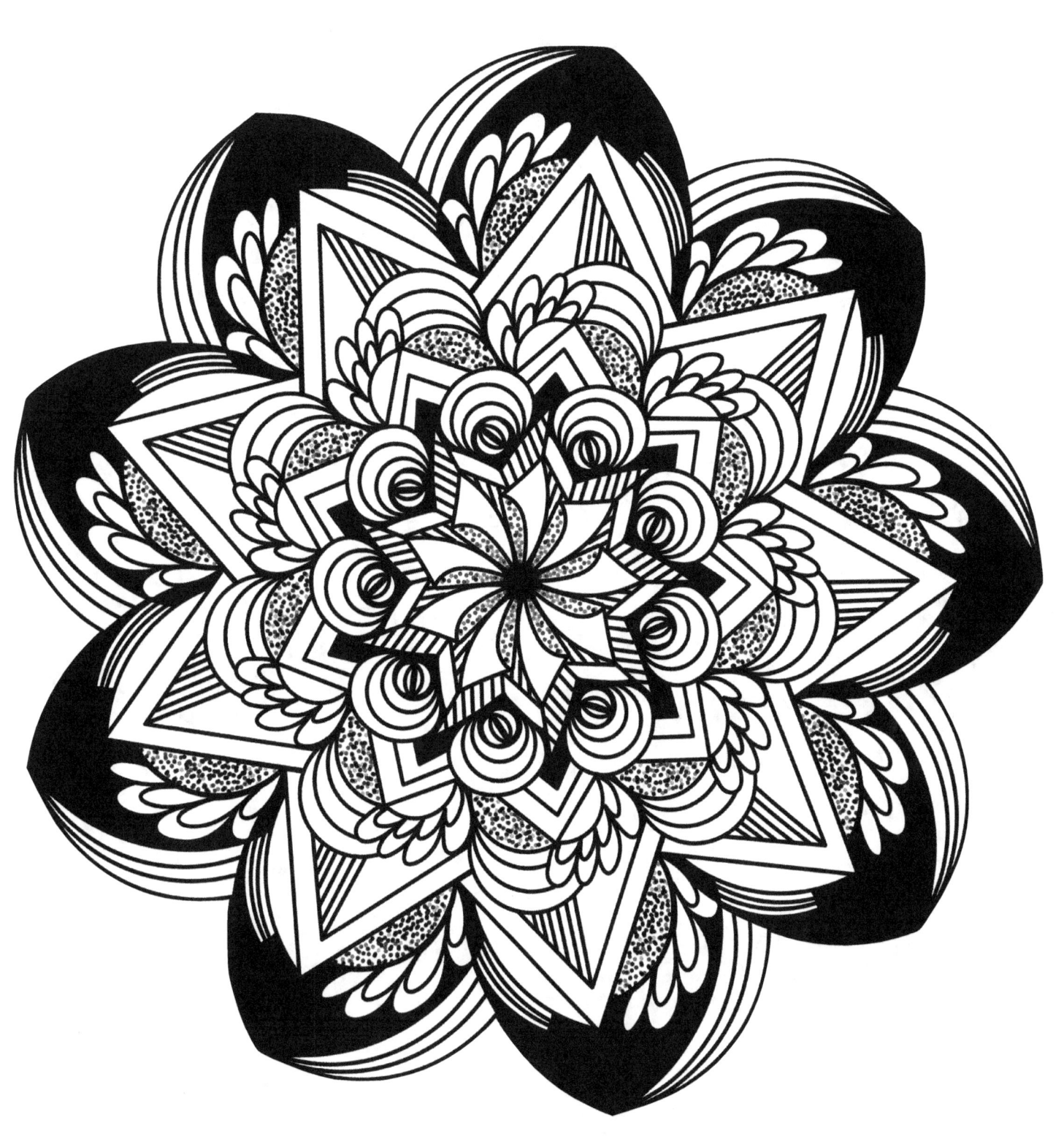

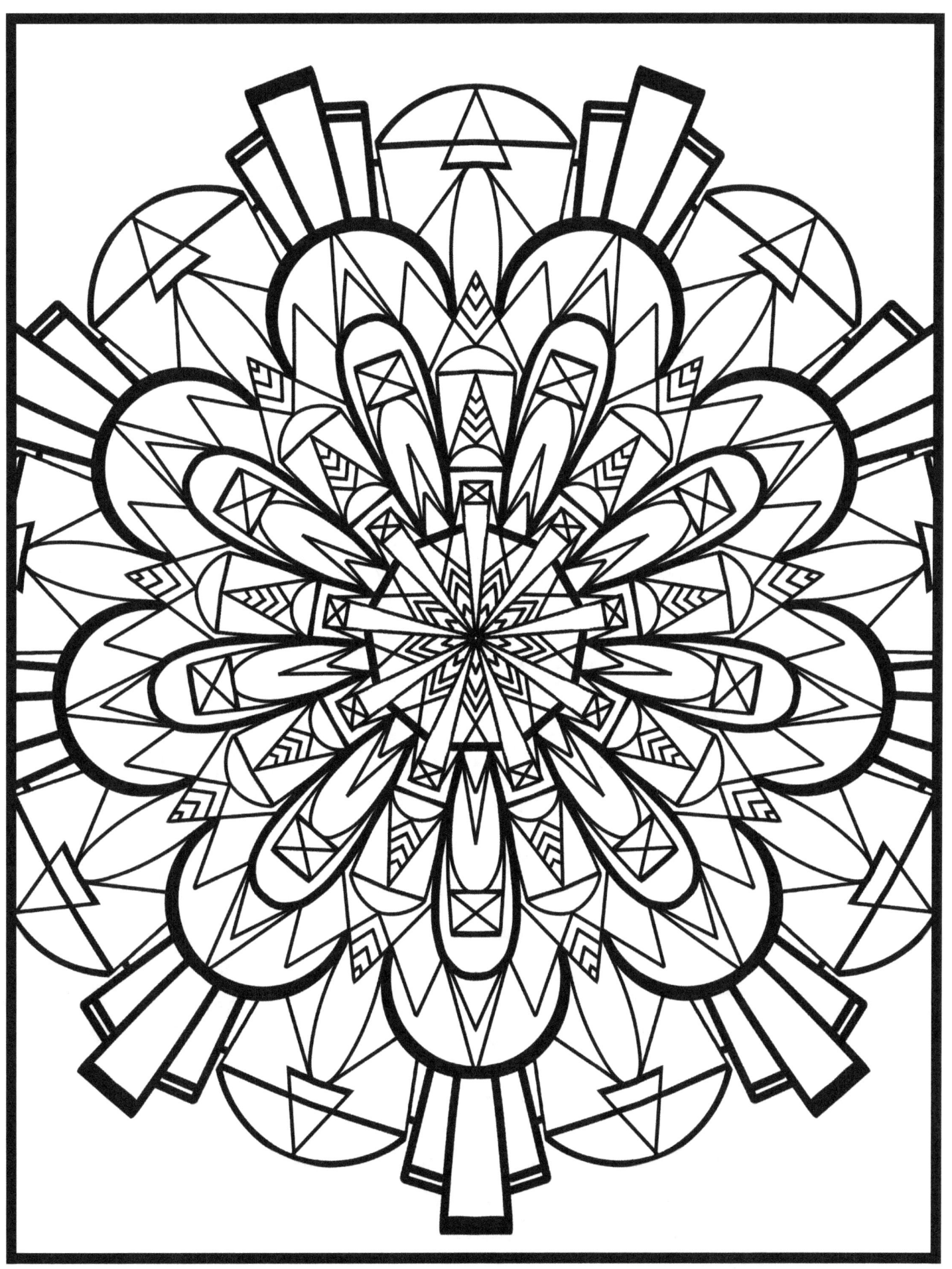

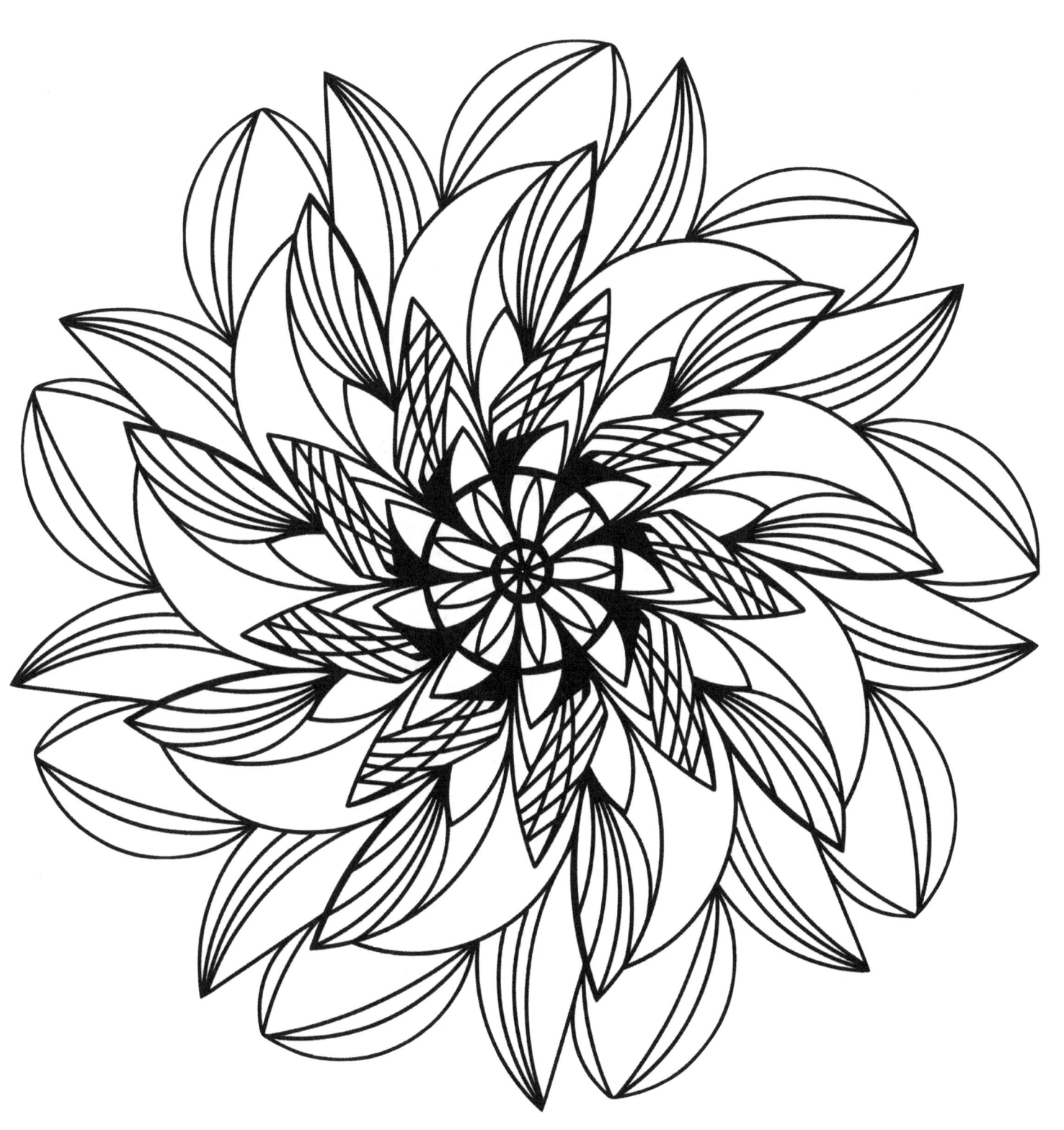

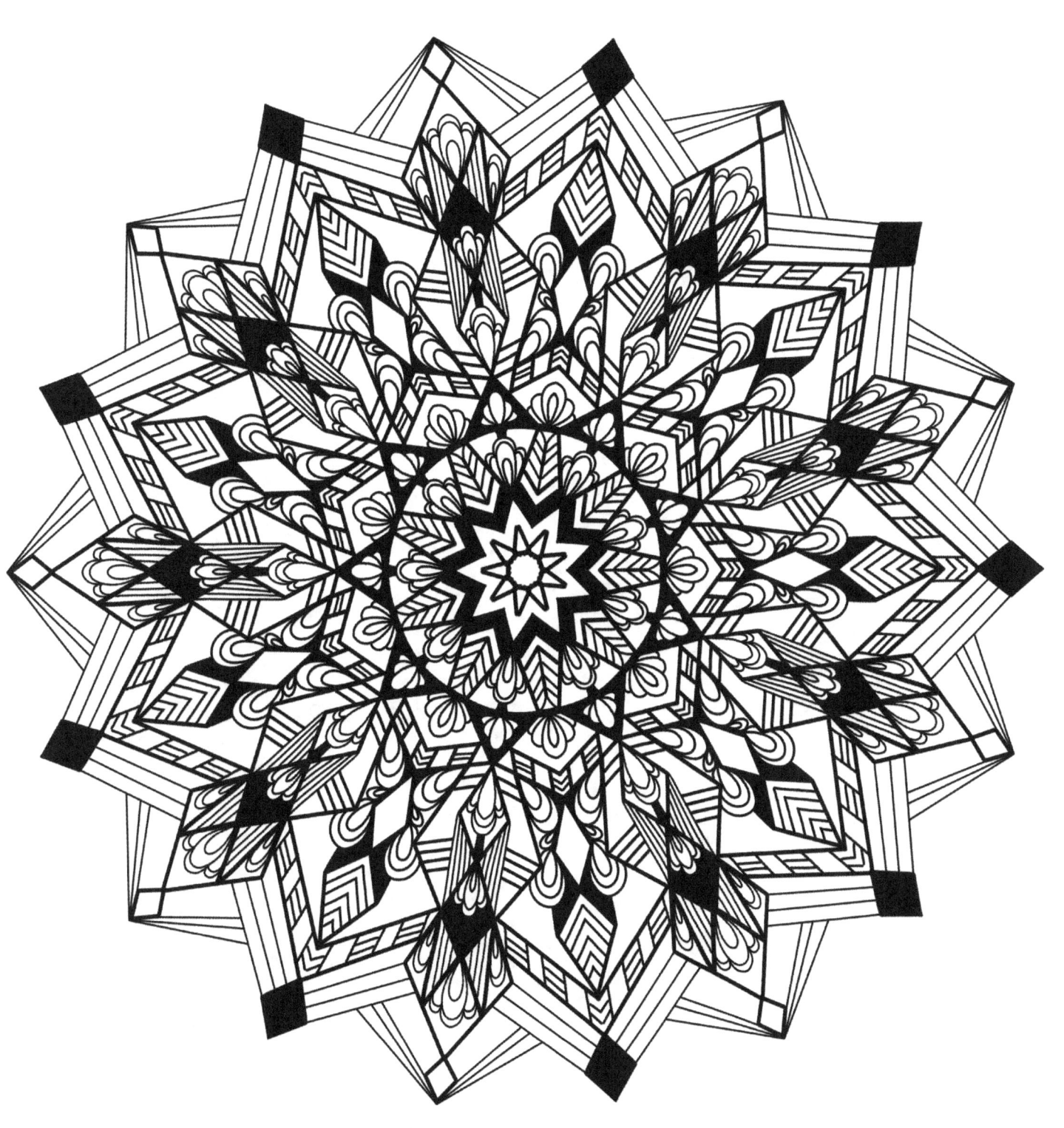

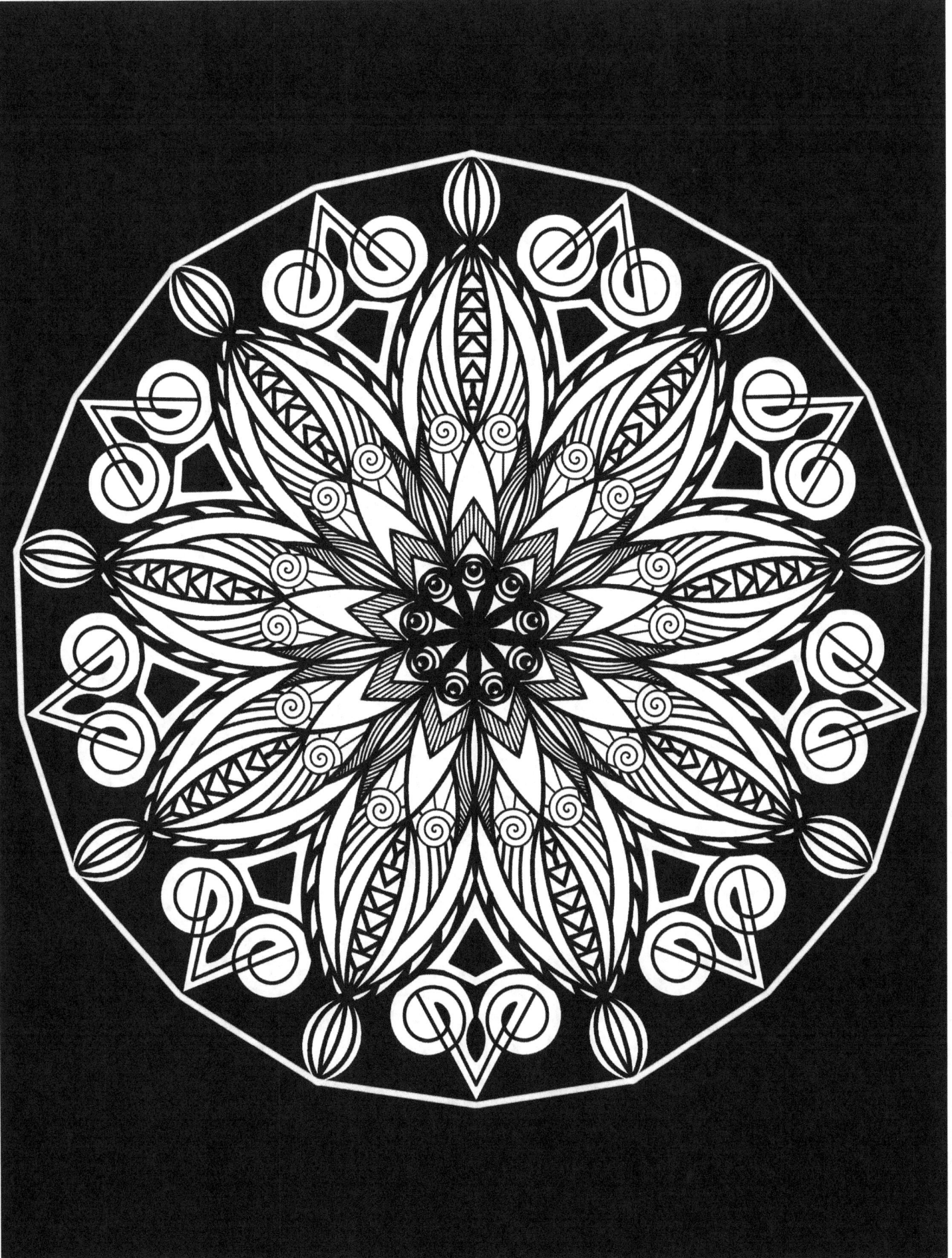

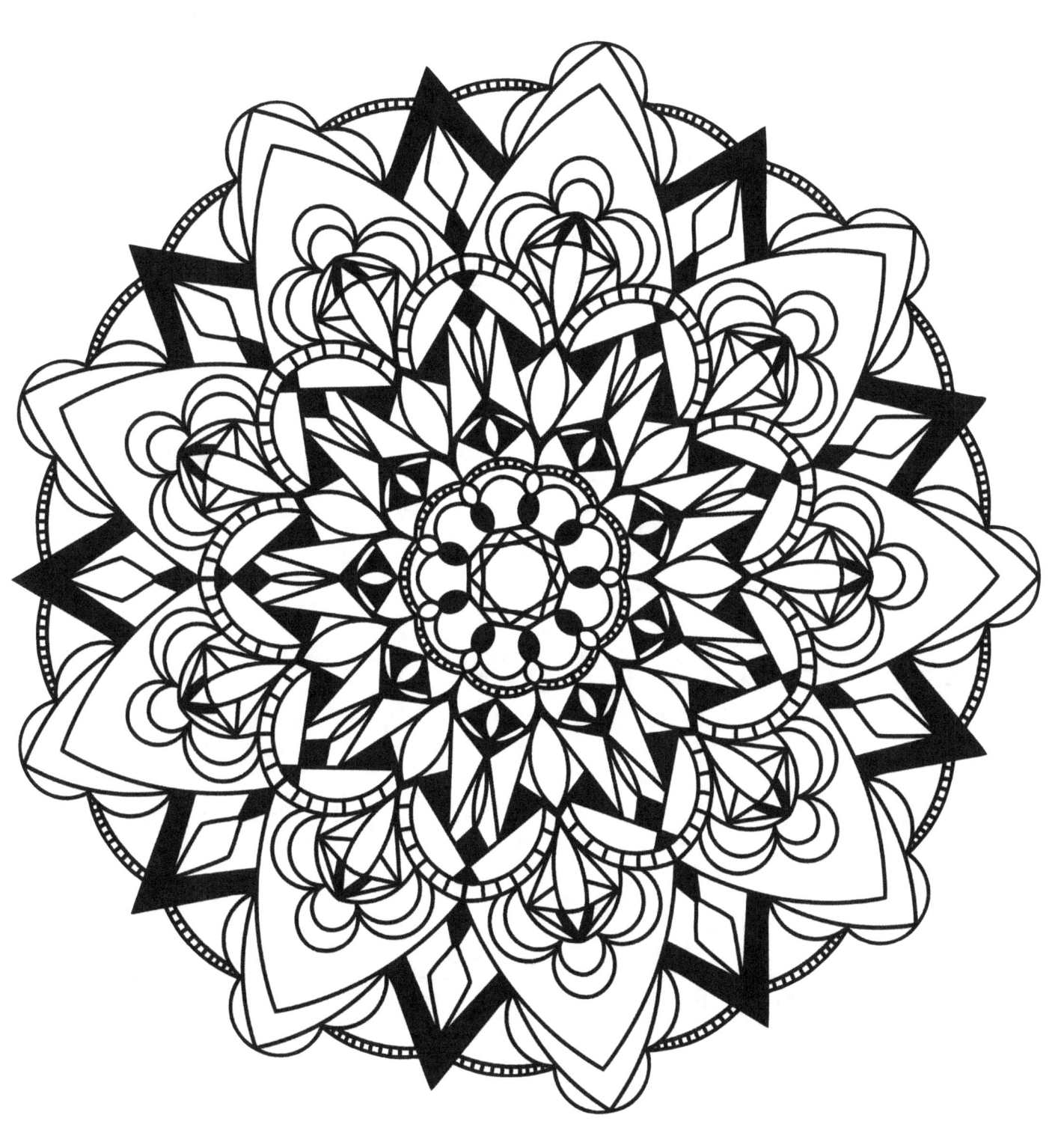

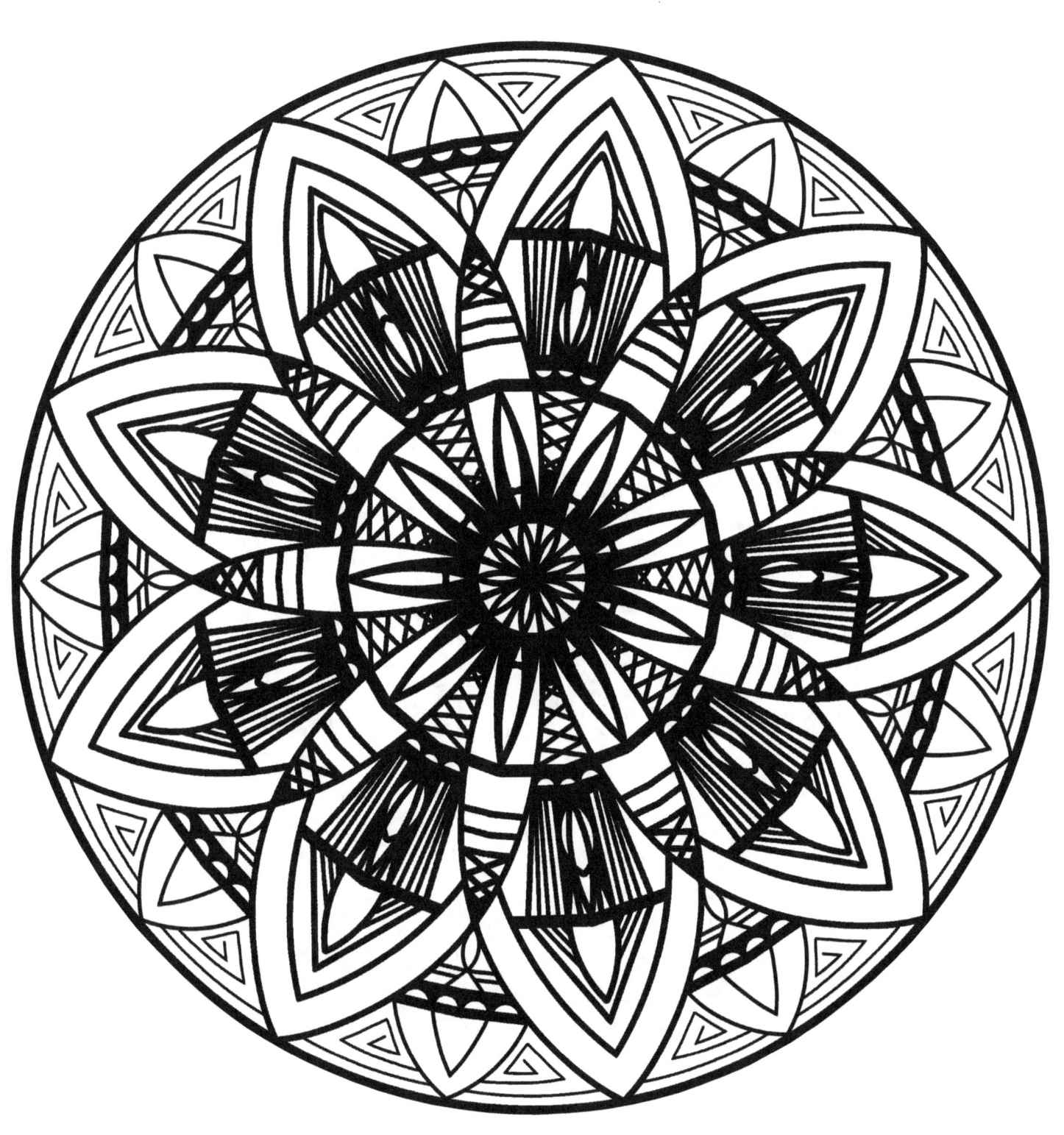

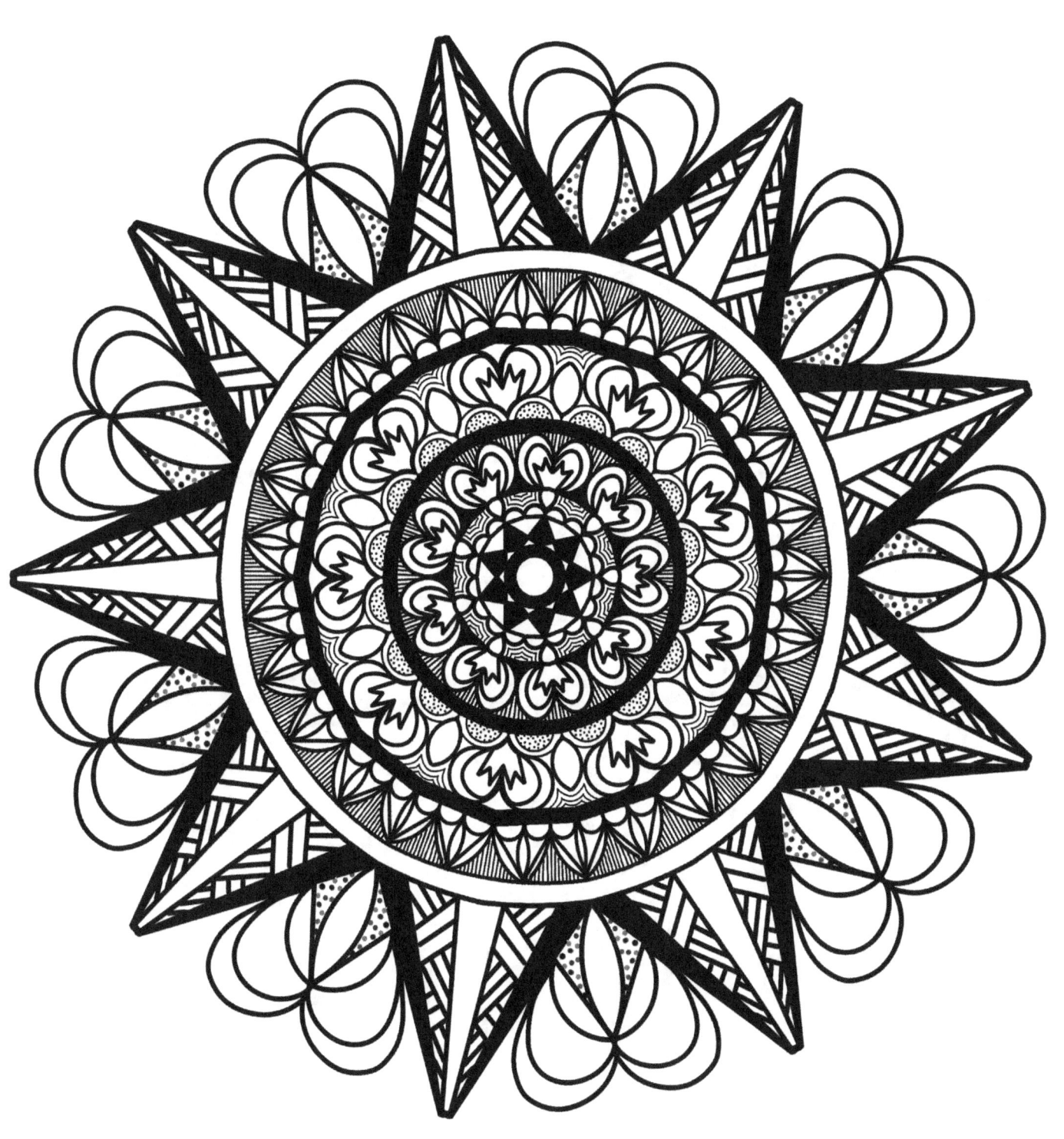

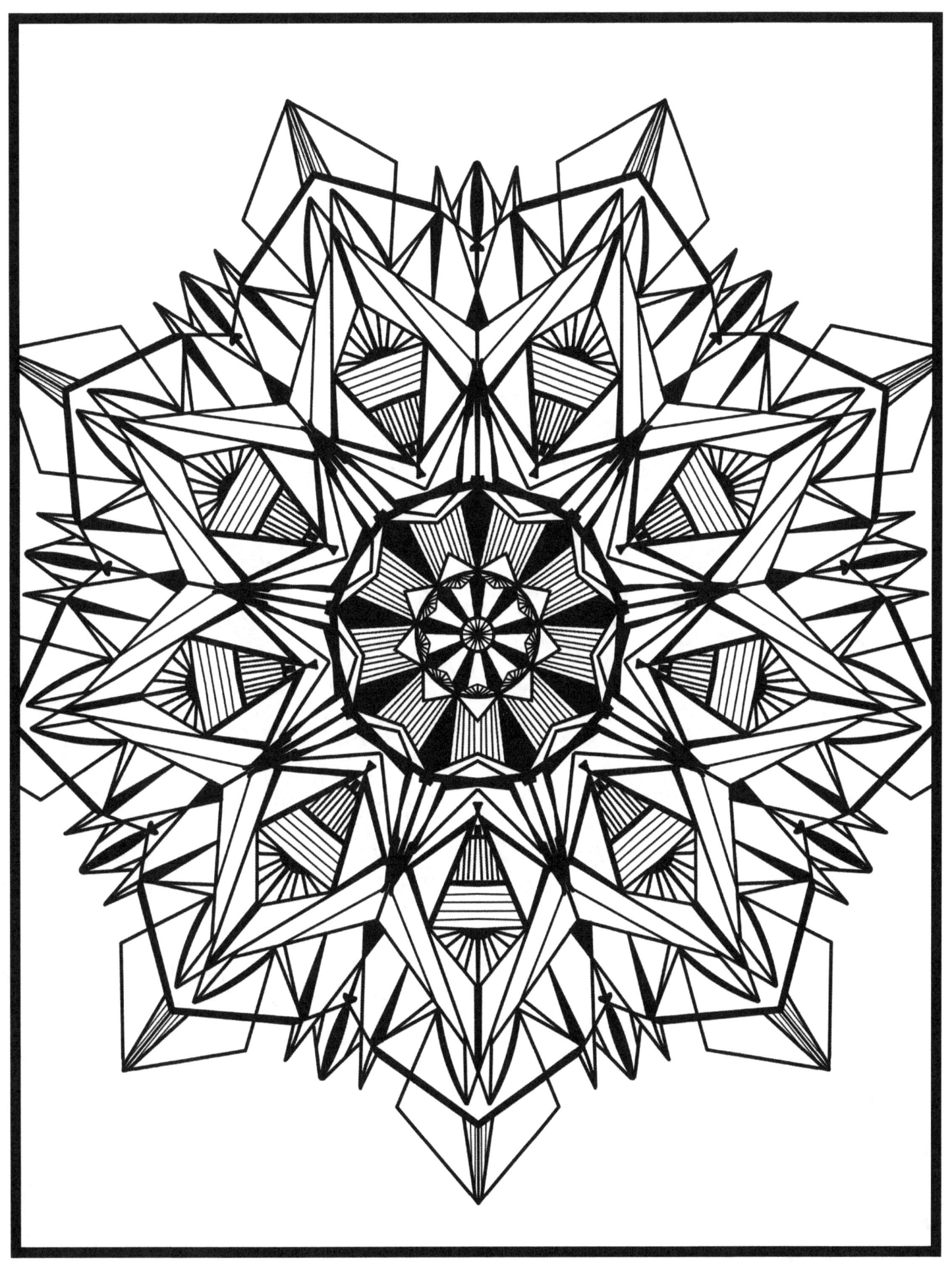

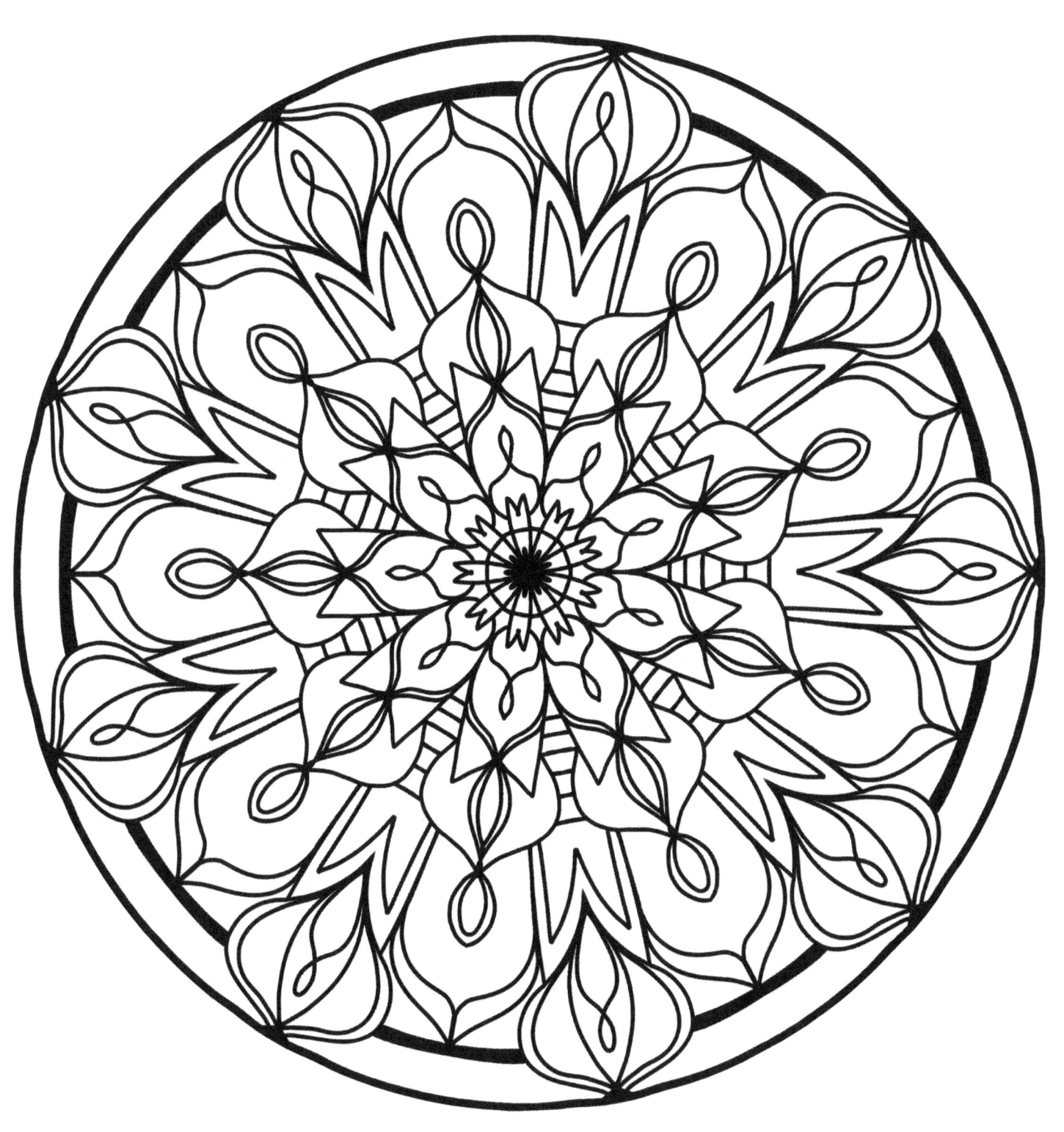

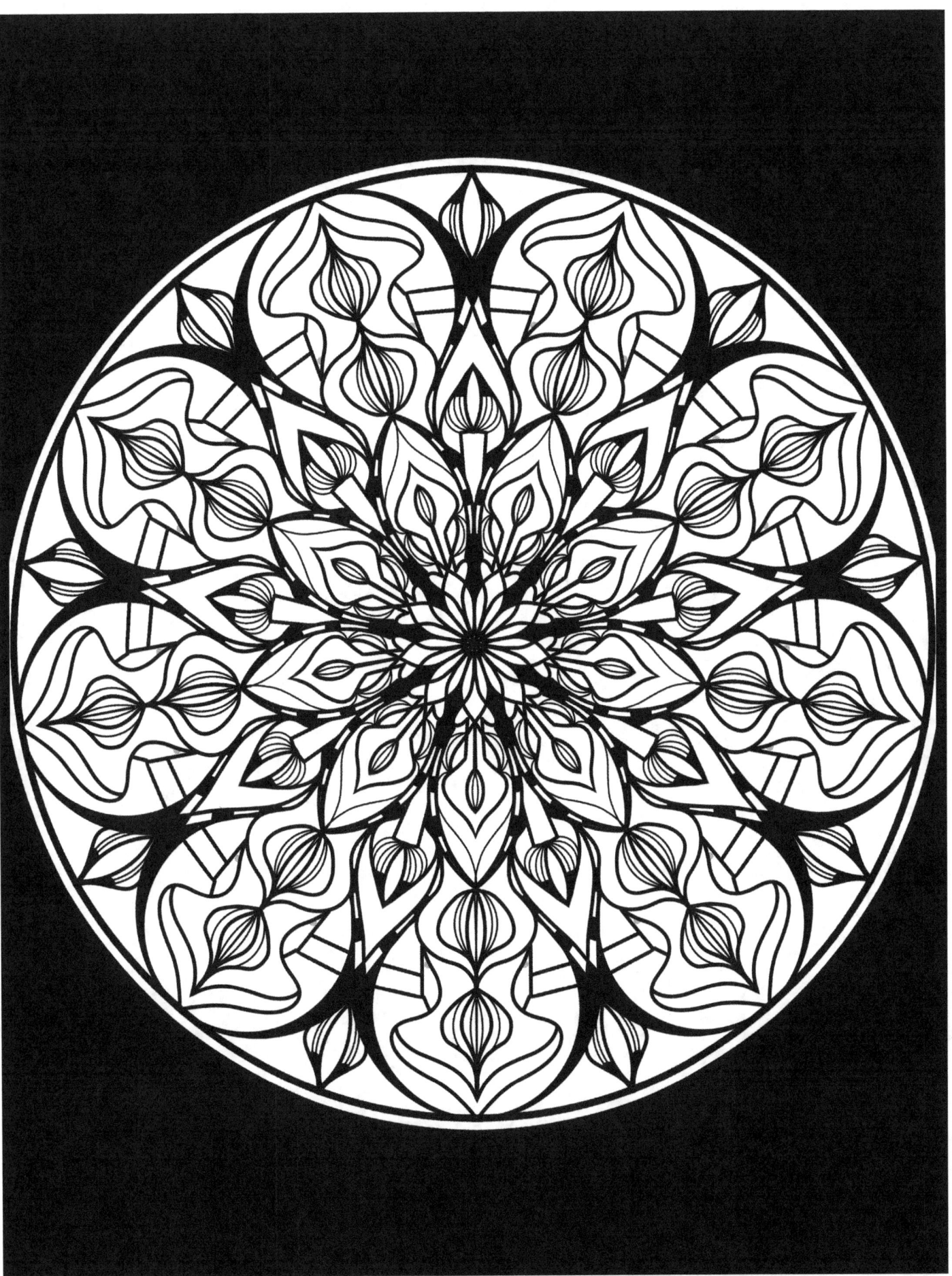

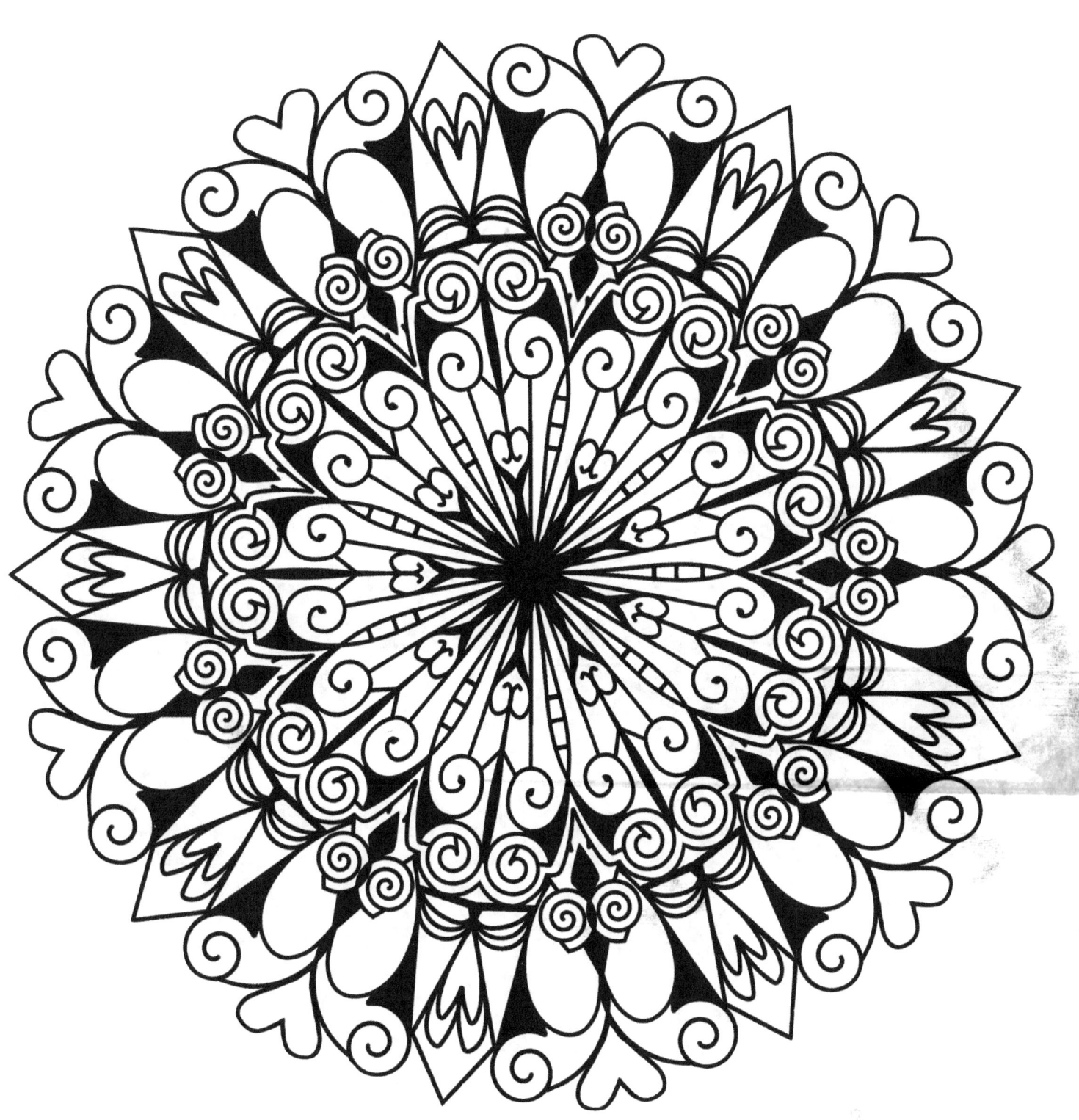

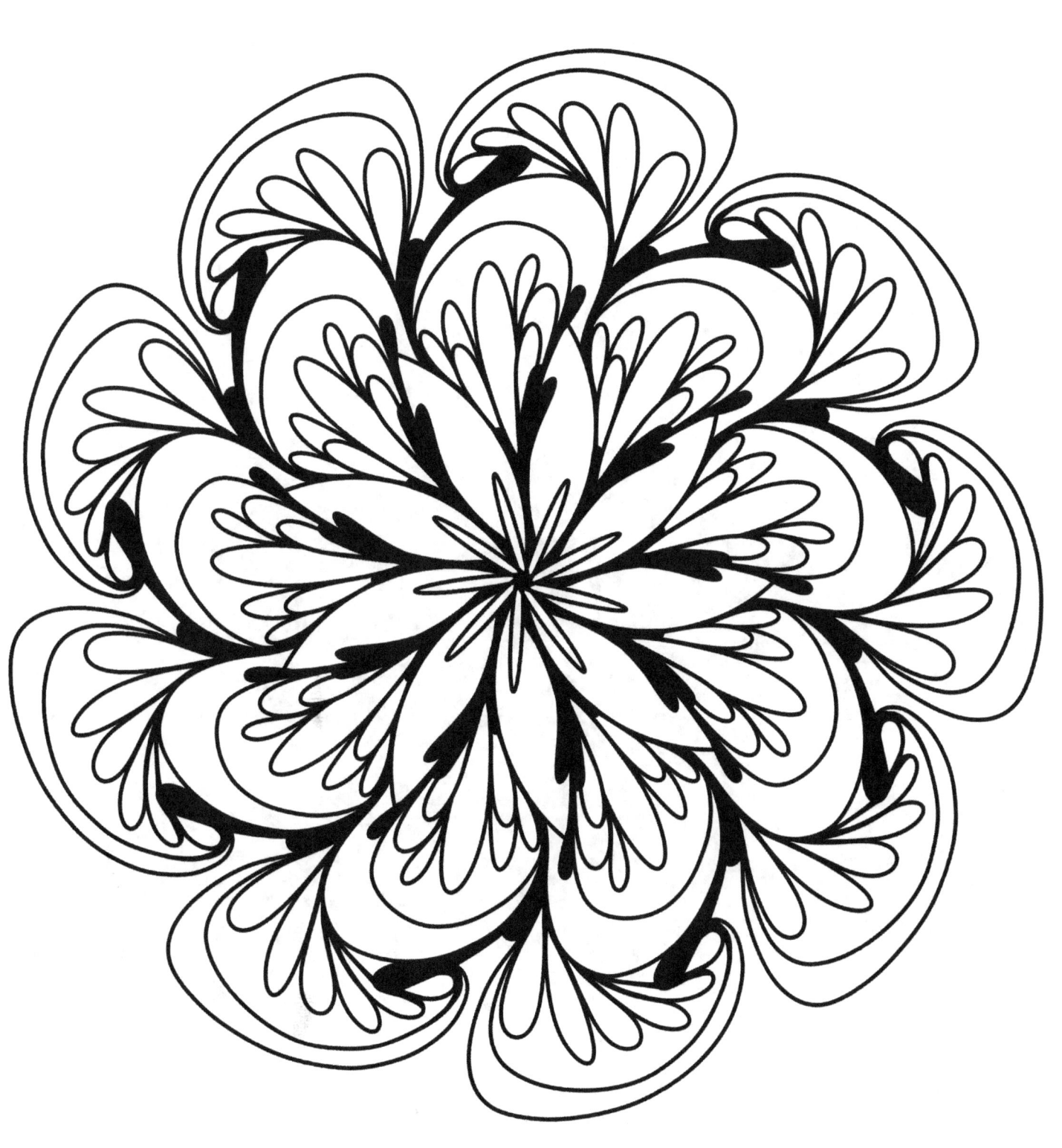

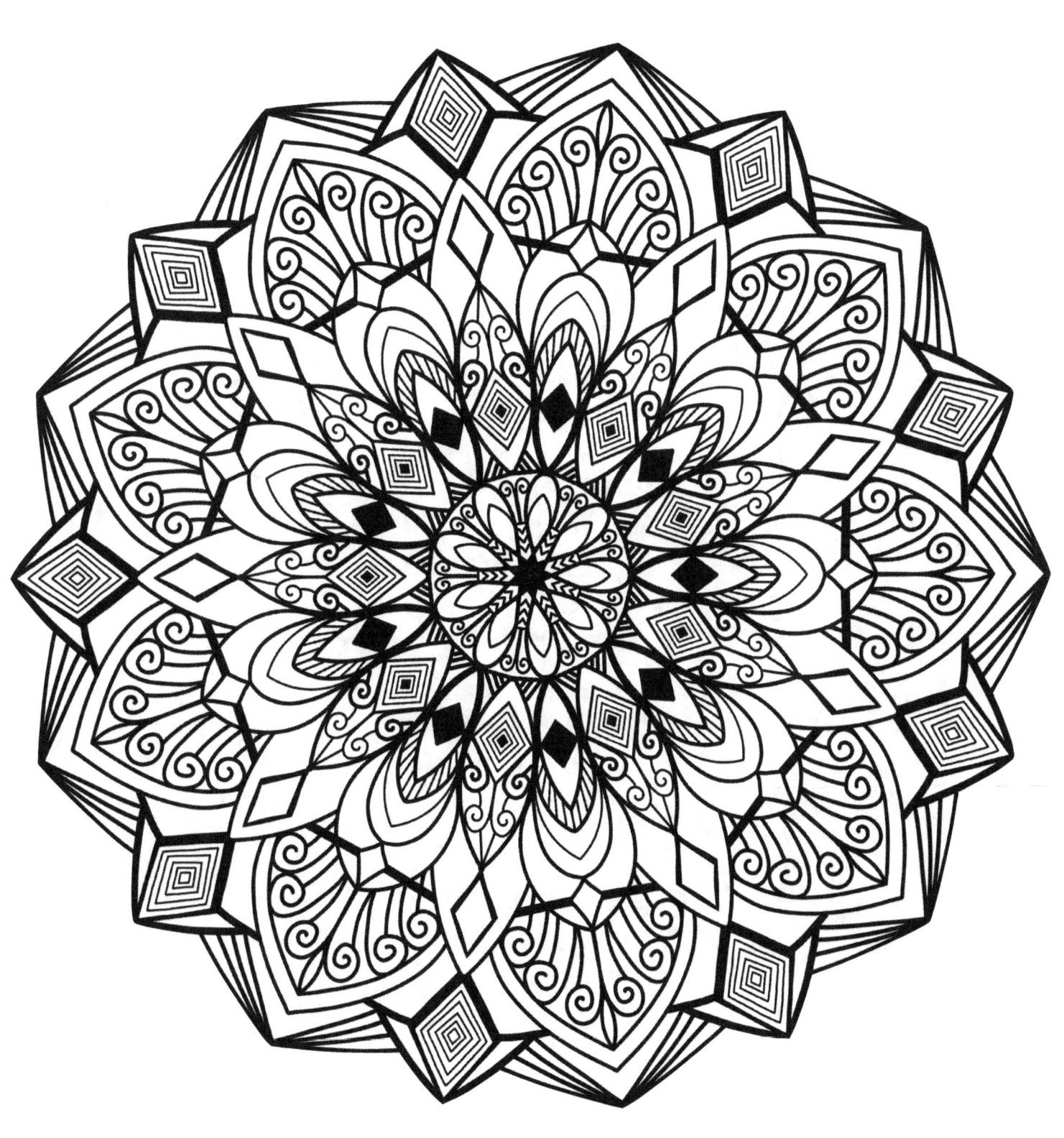

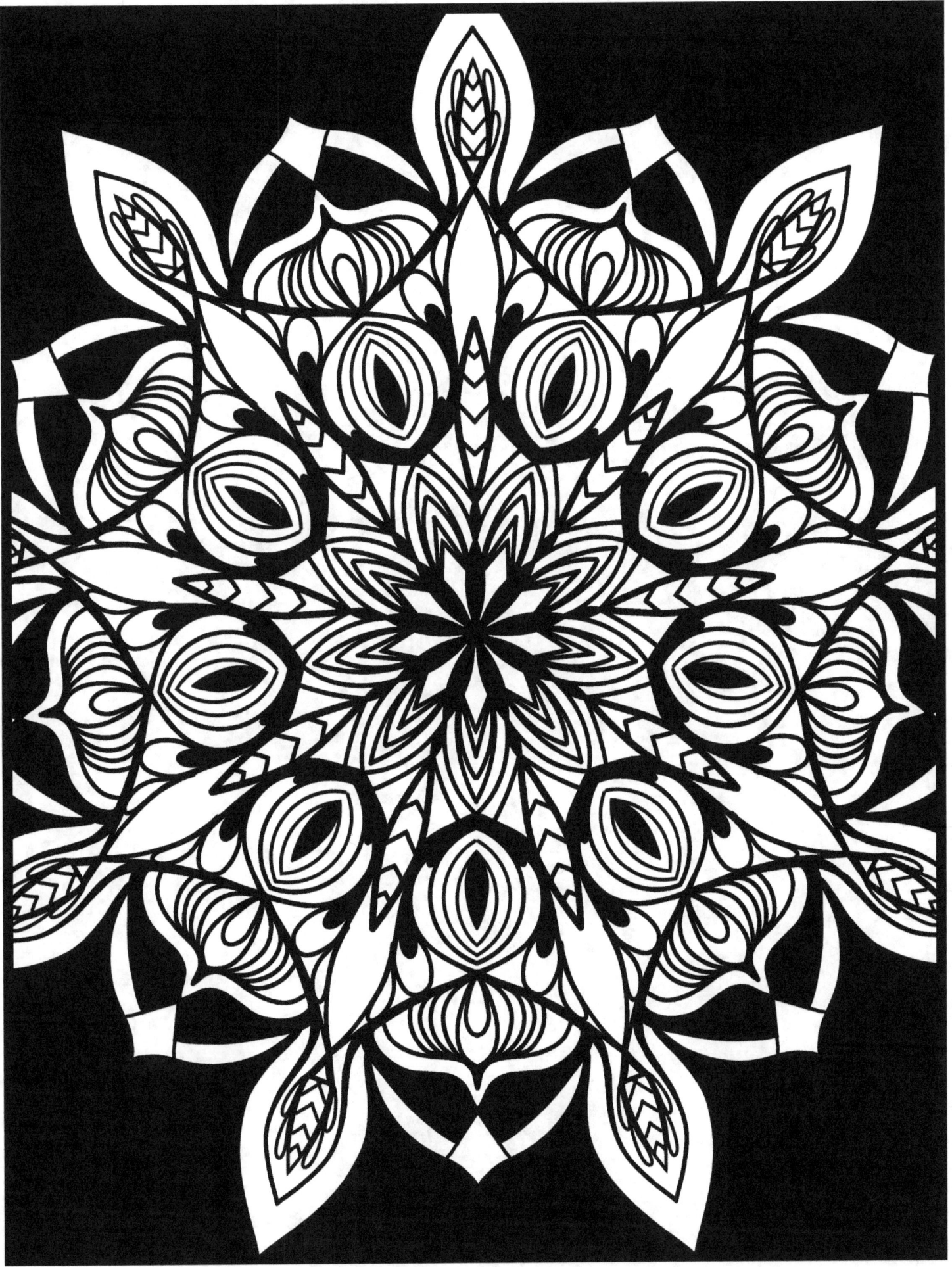

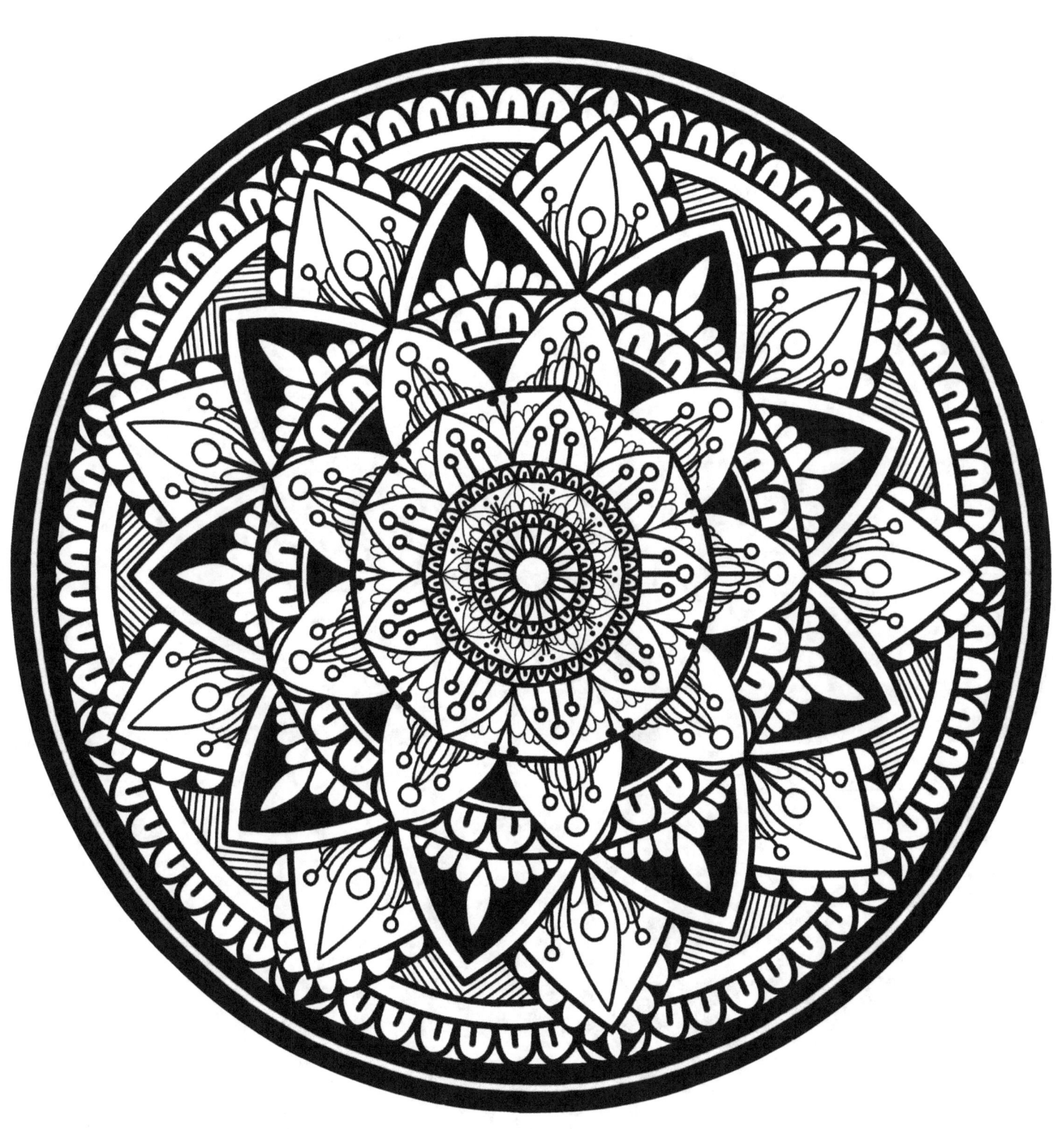

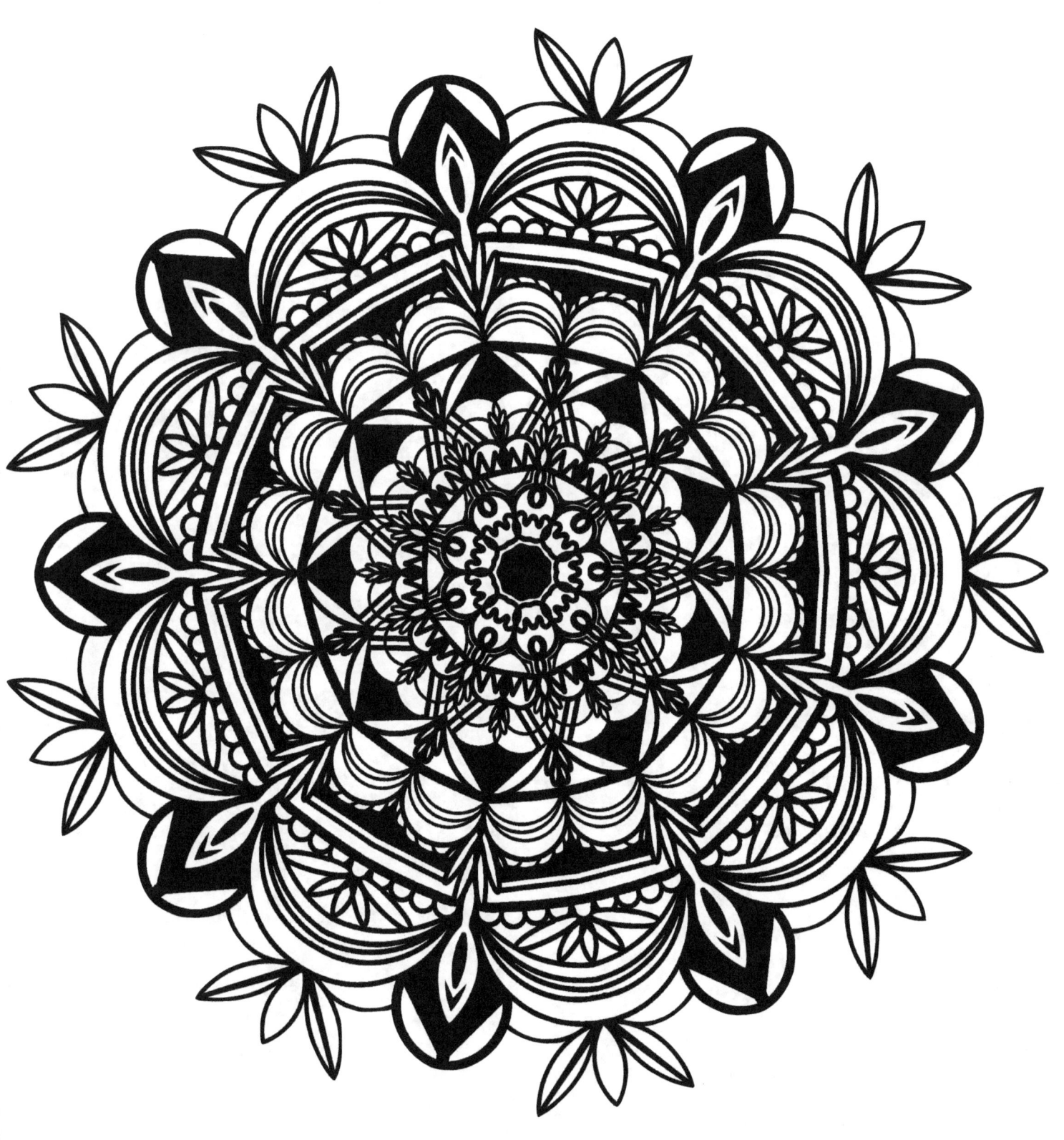

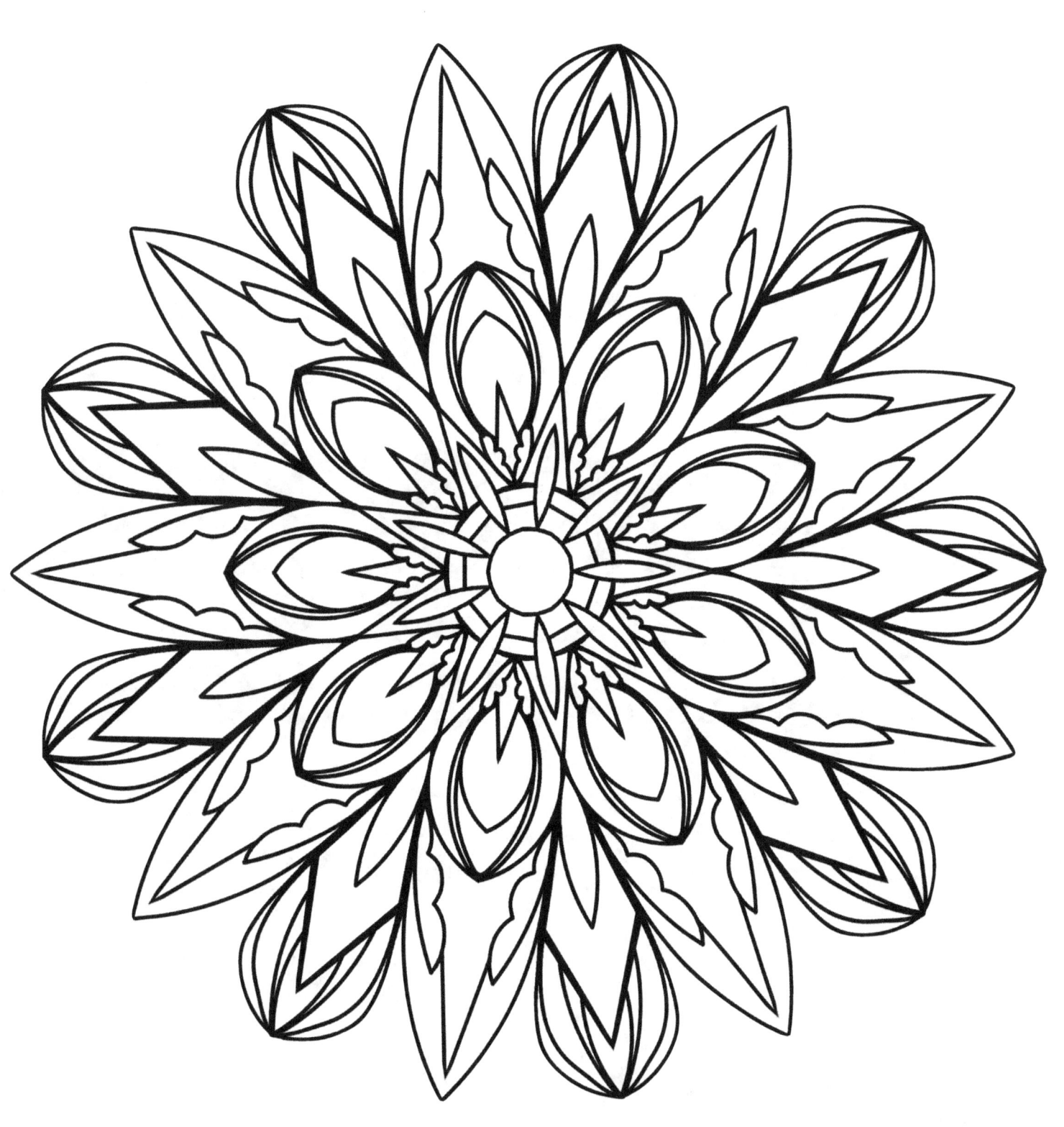

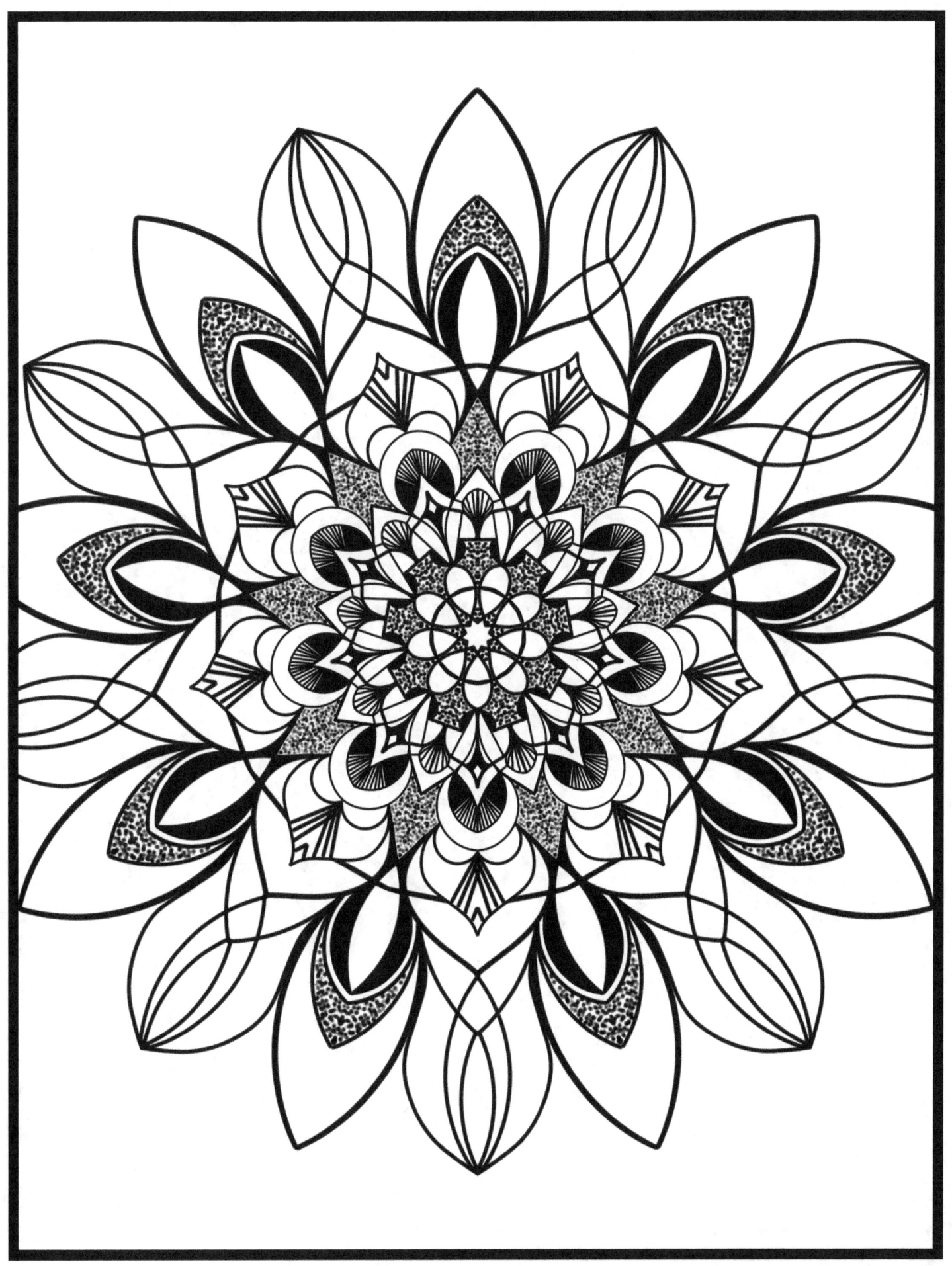

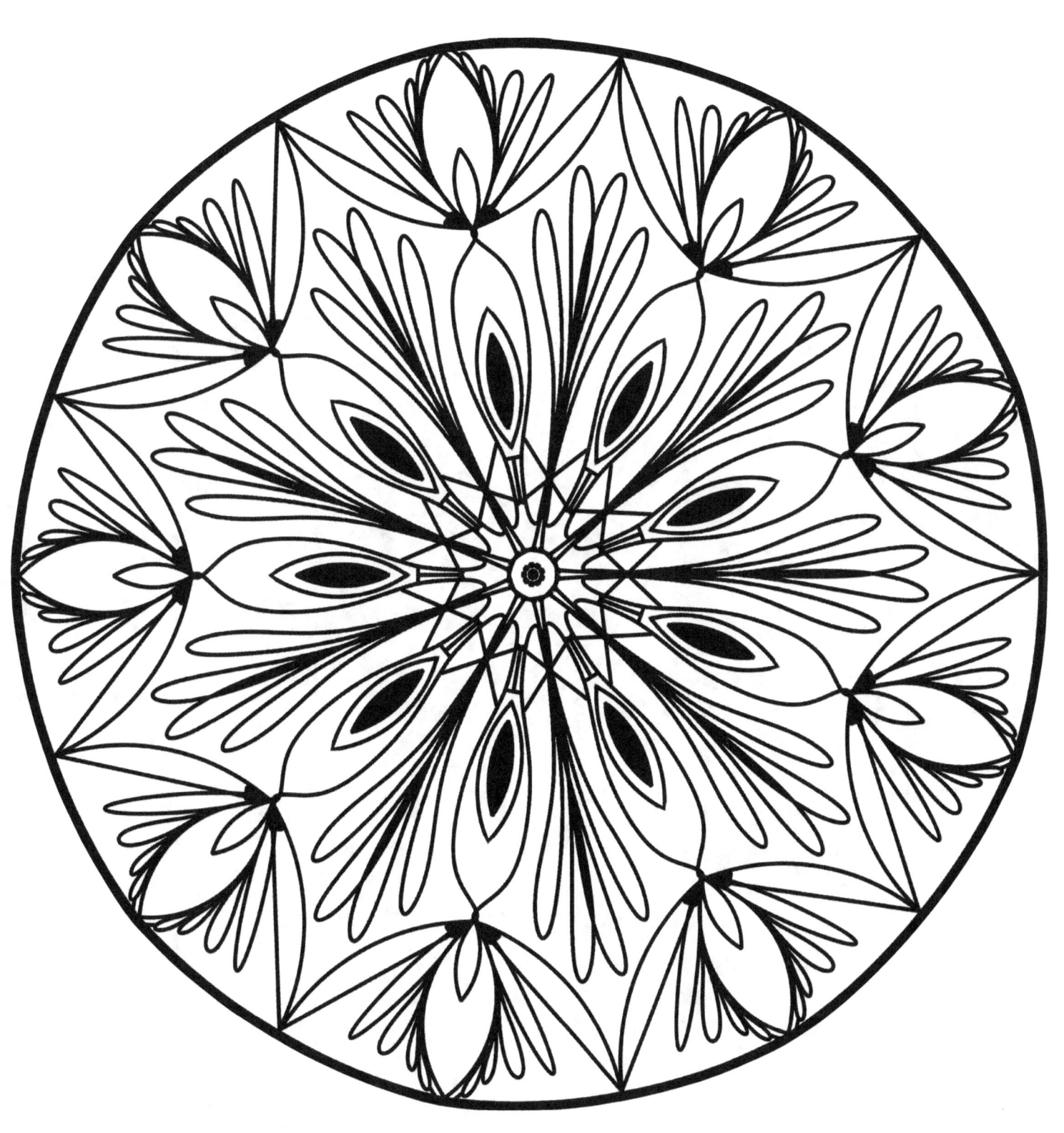

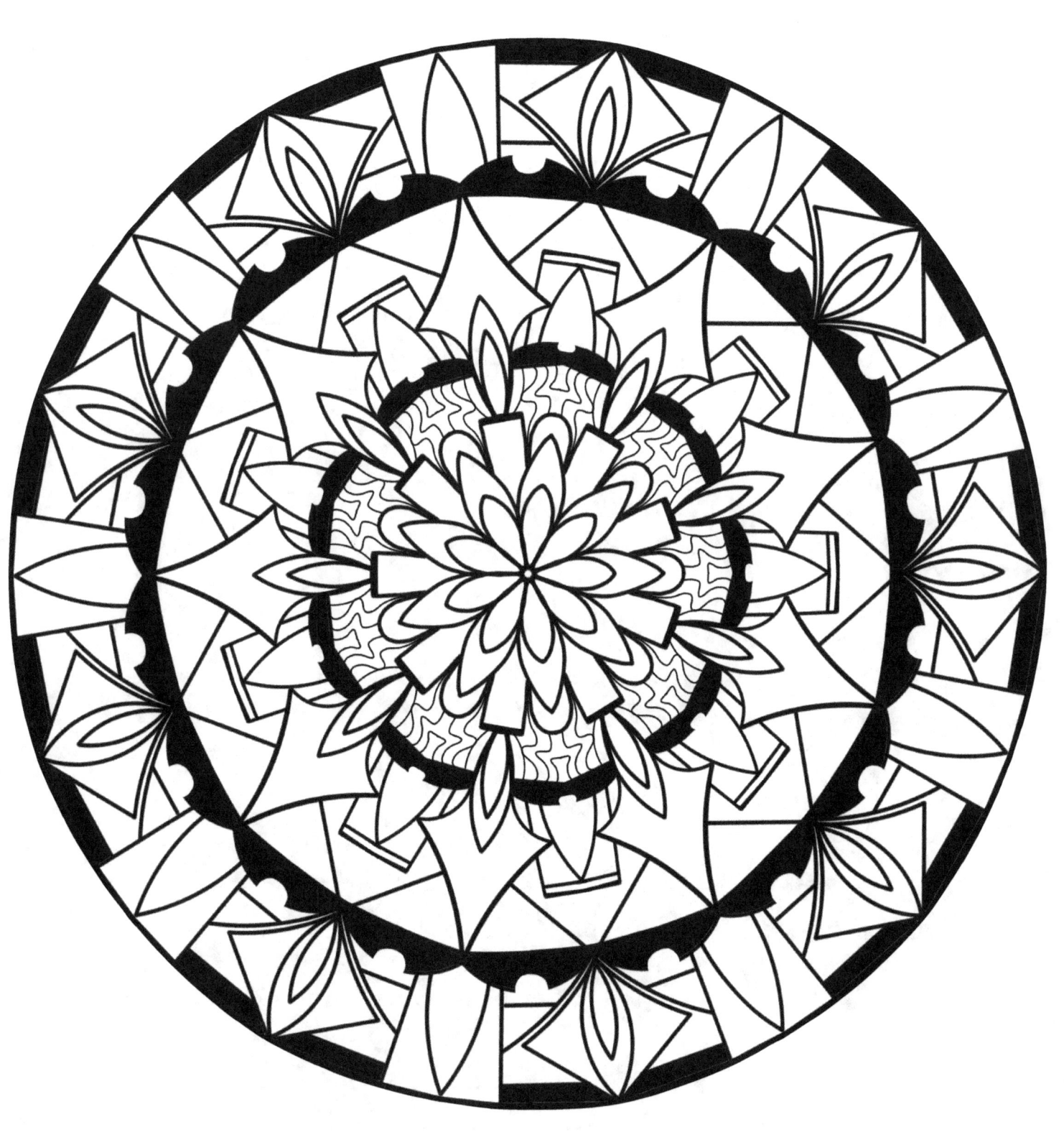

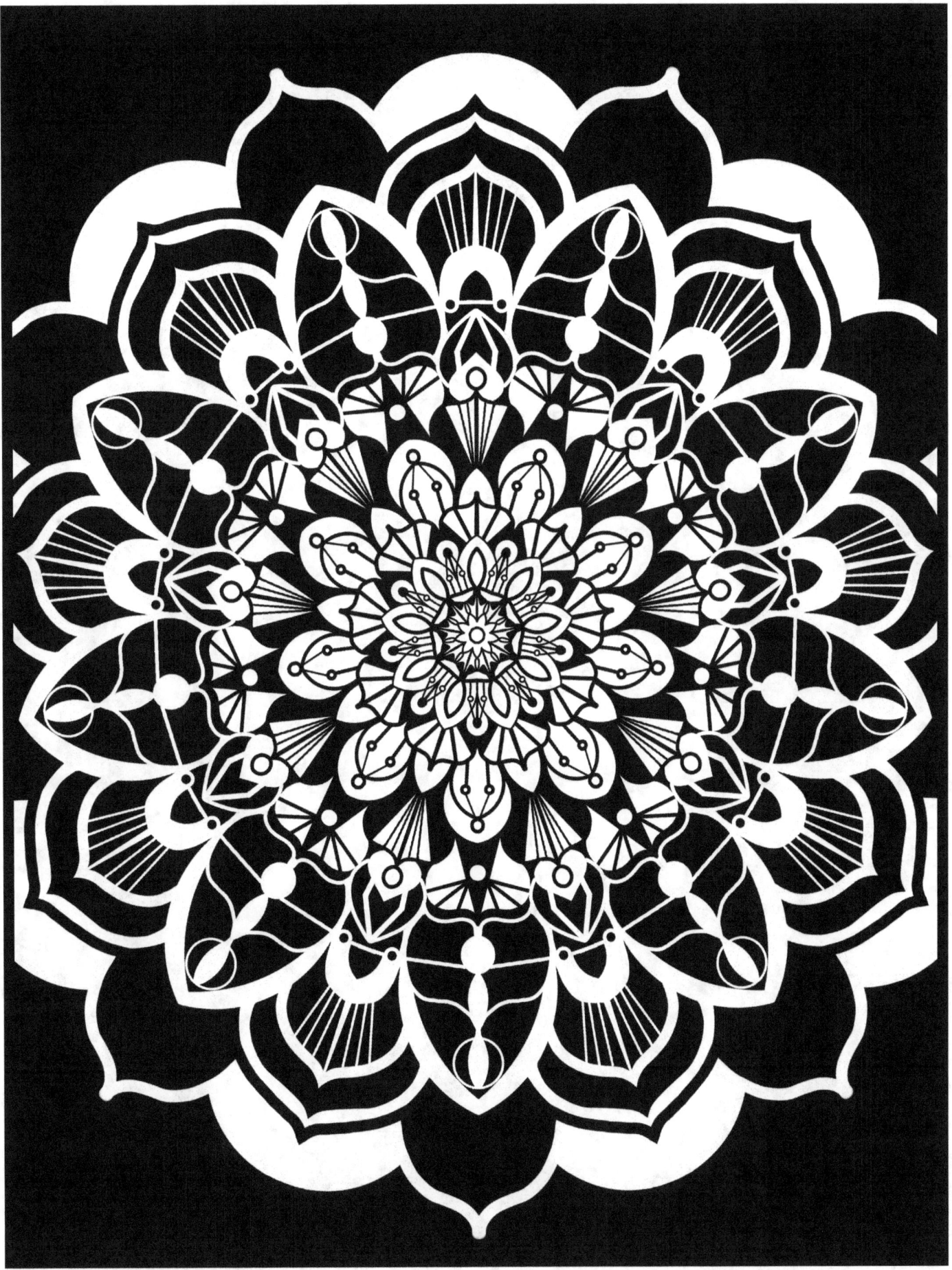

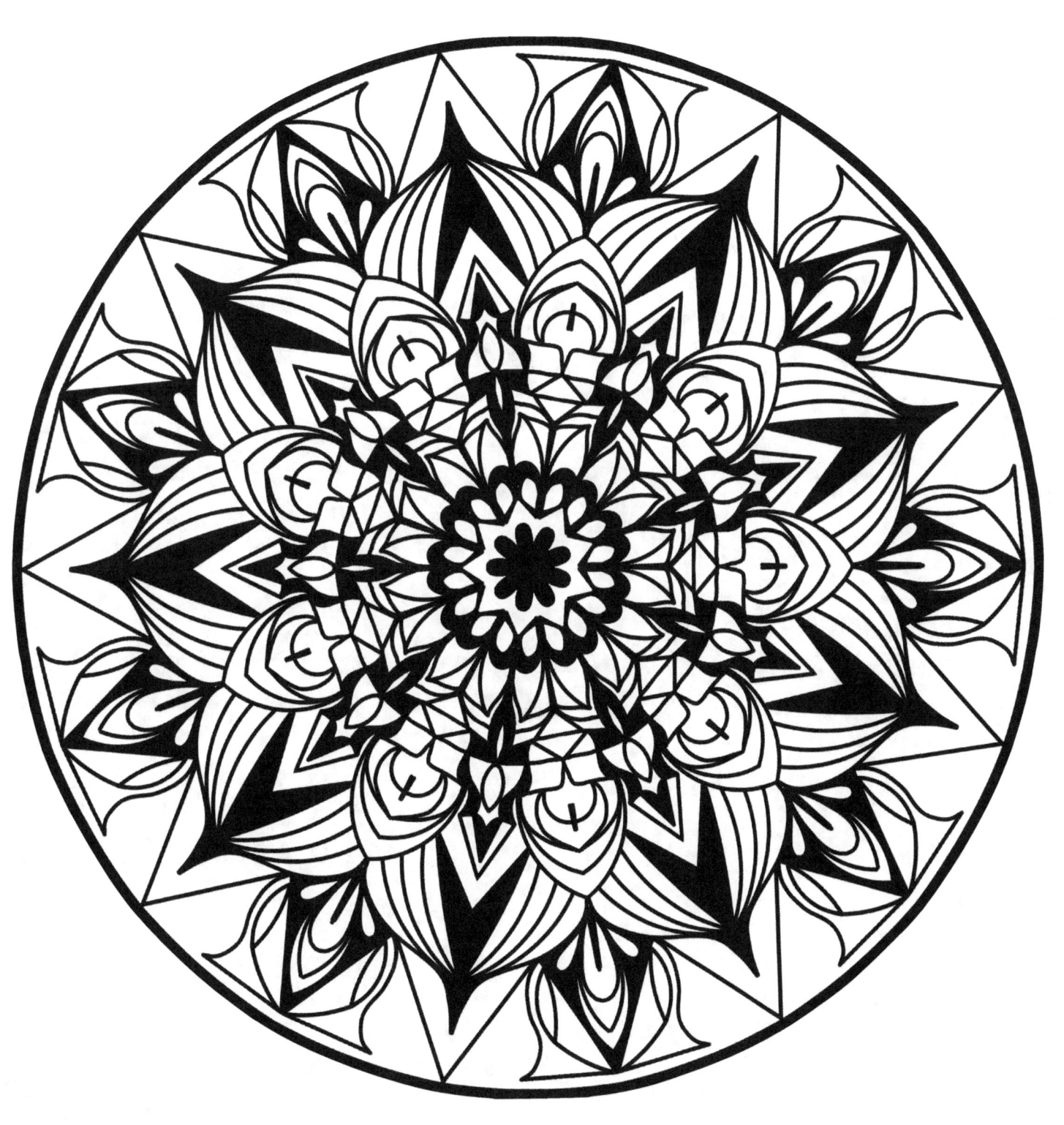

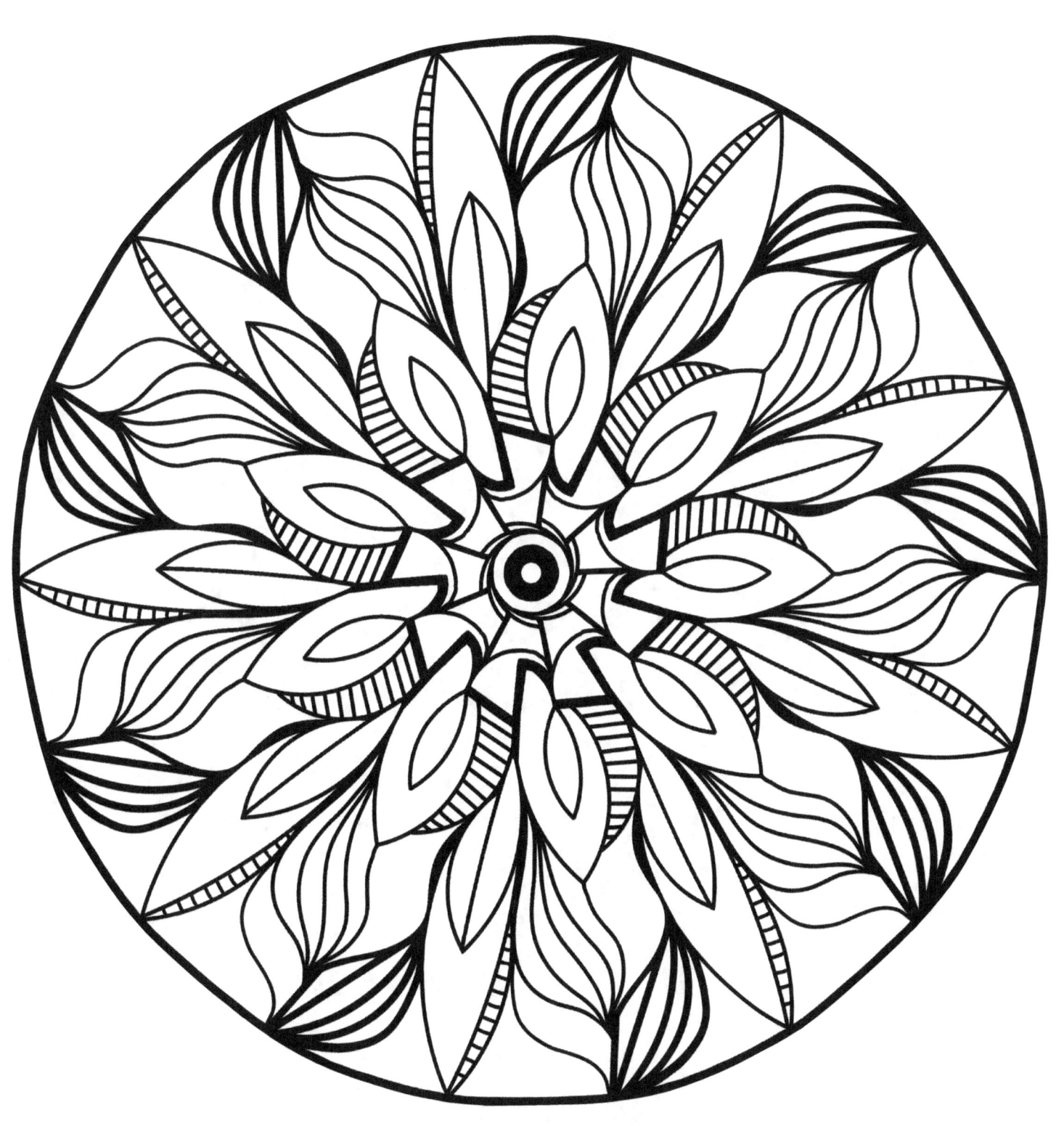

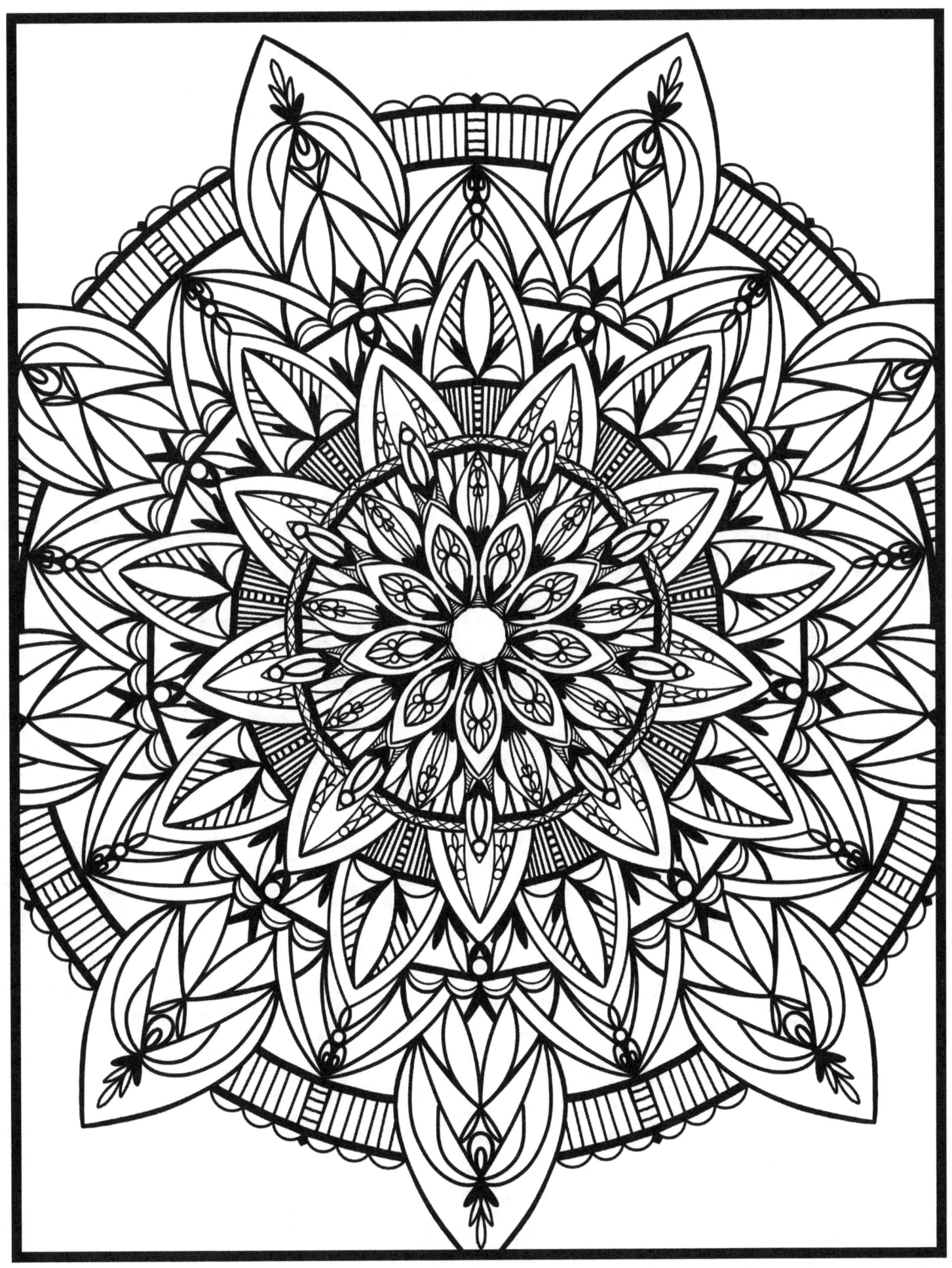

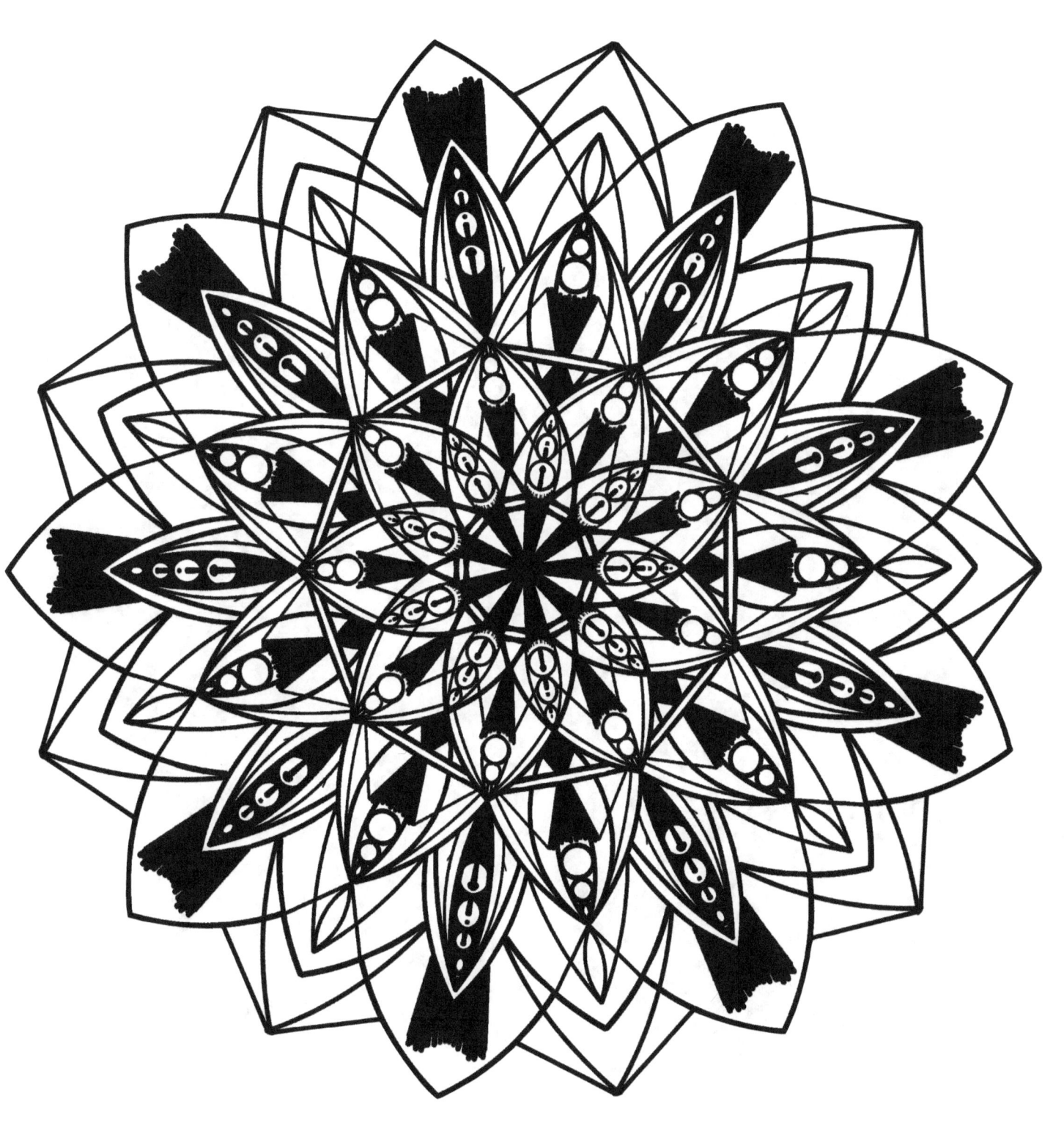

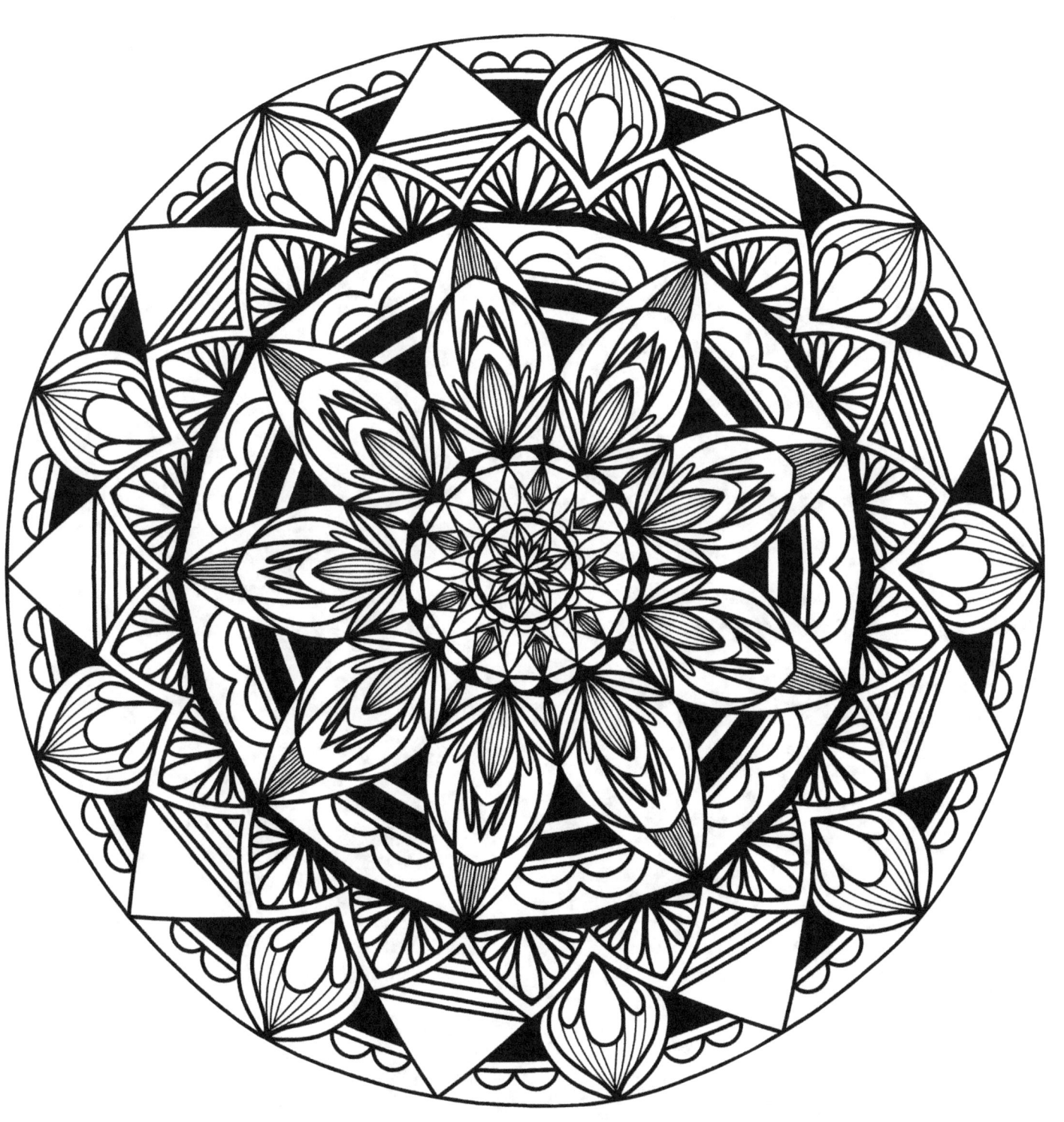

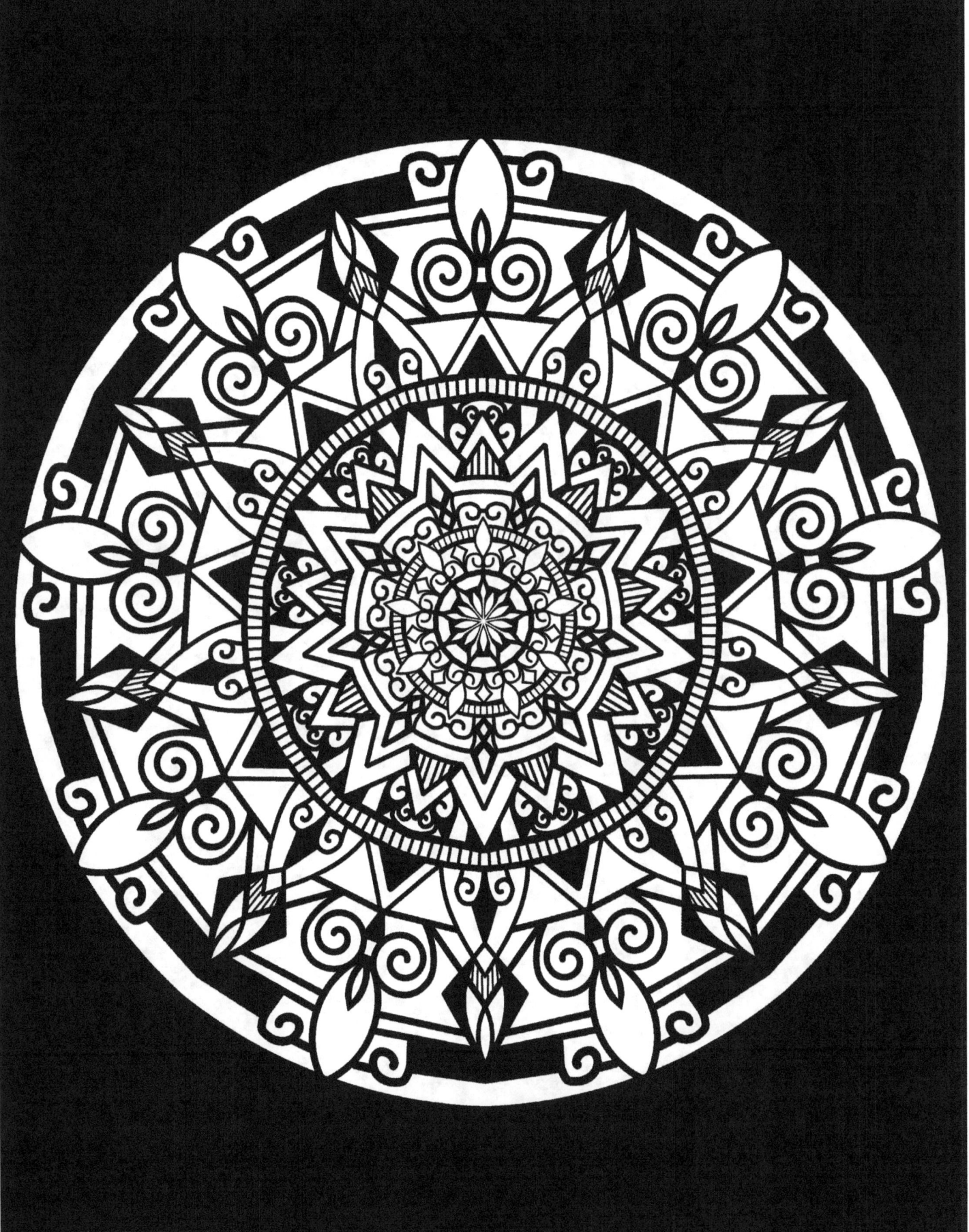

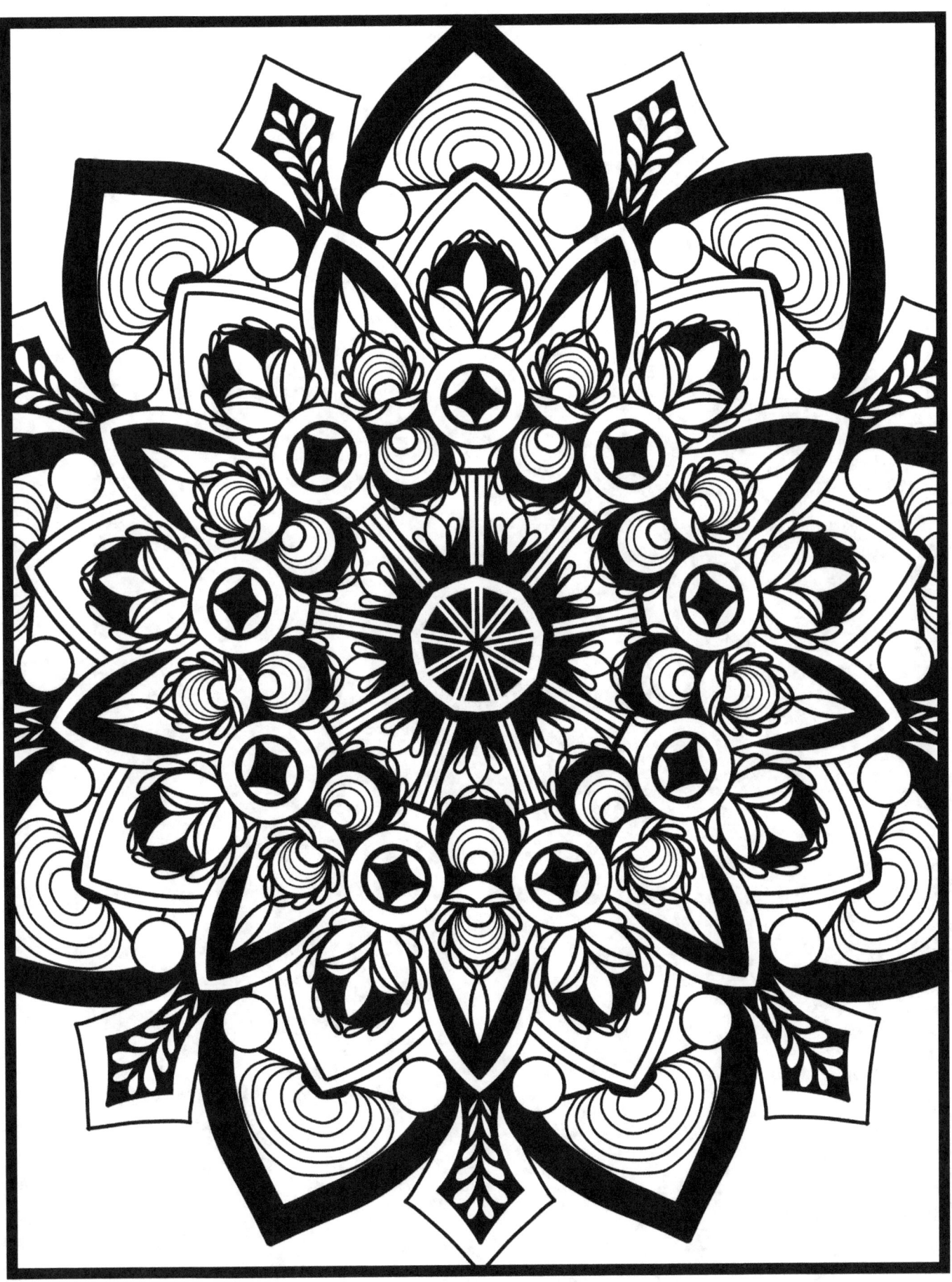

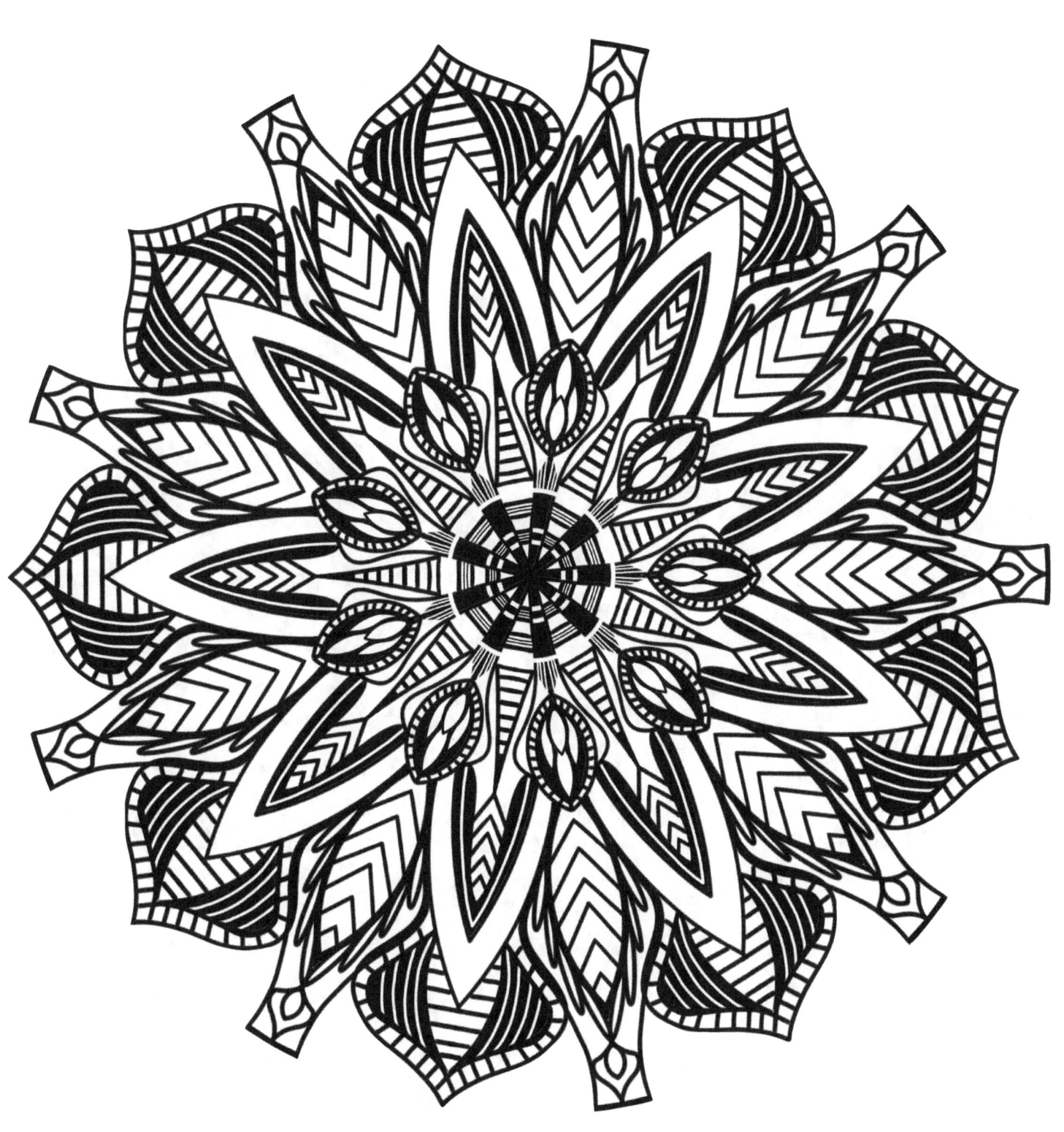

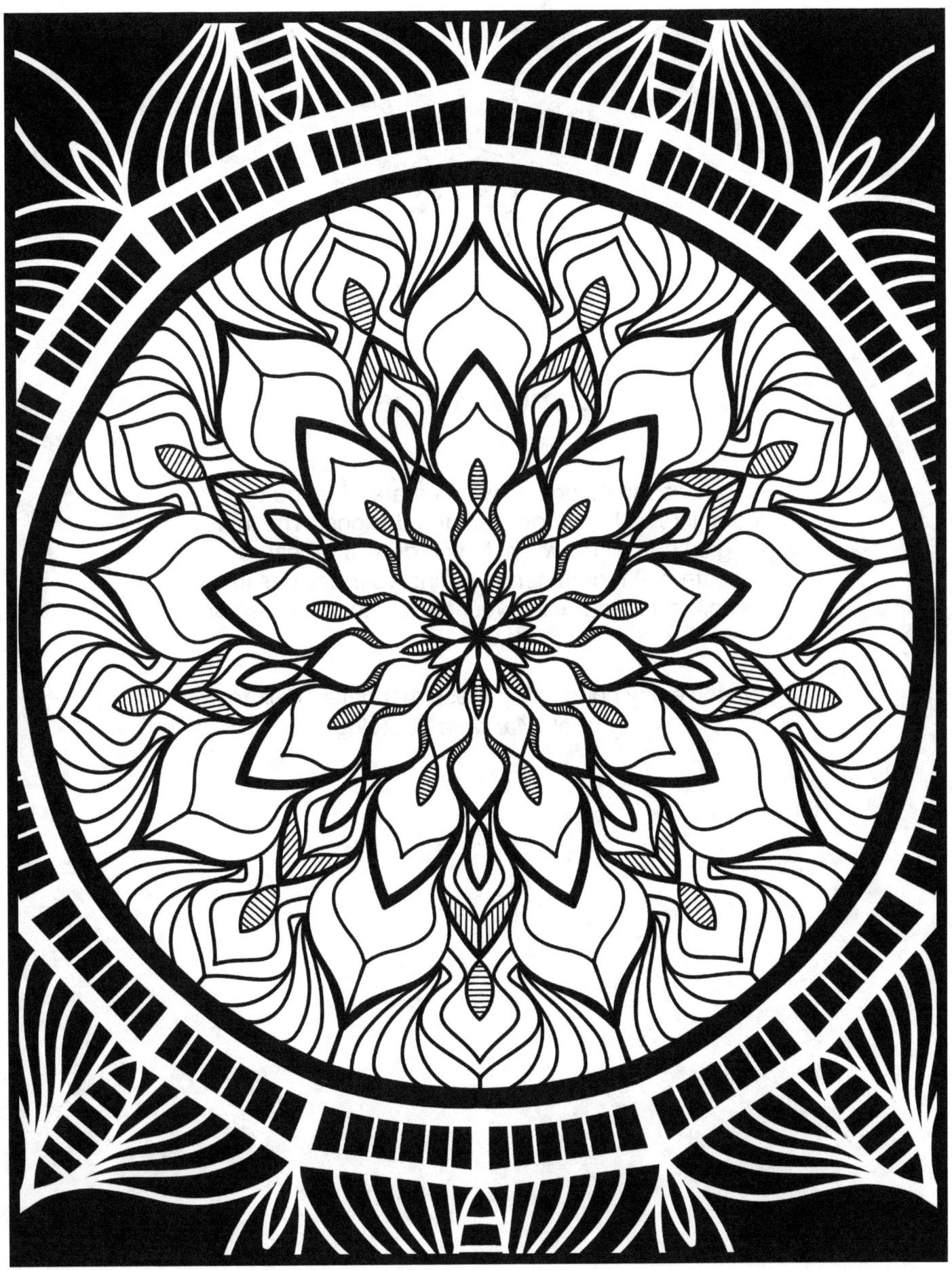

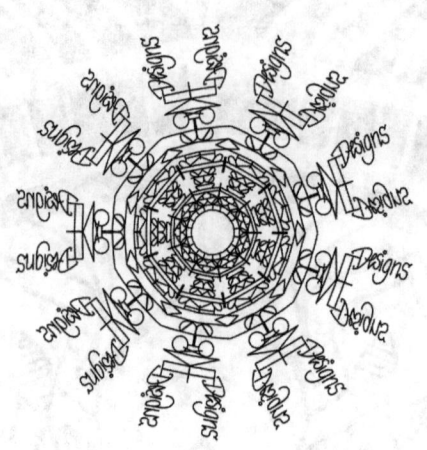

Bonus Mandalas

These ten mandalas were created for you to complete with your own unique designs. The light gray guidelines will help you draw a repeated pattern. I recommend starting your designs in pencil and then tracing your lines with black pen or marker.

If you enjoy completing these mandalas, look for my book *Mandala Drawing*

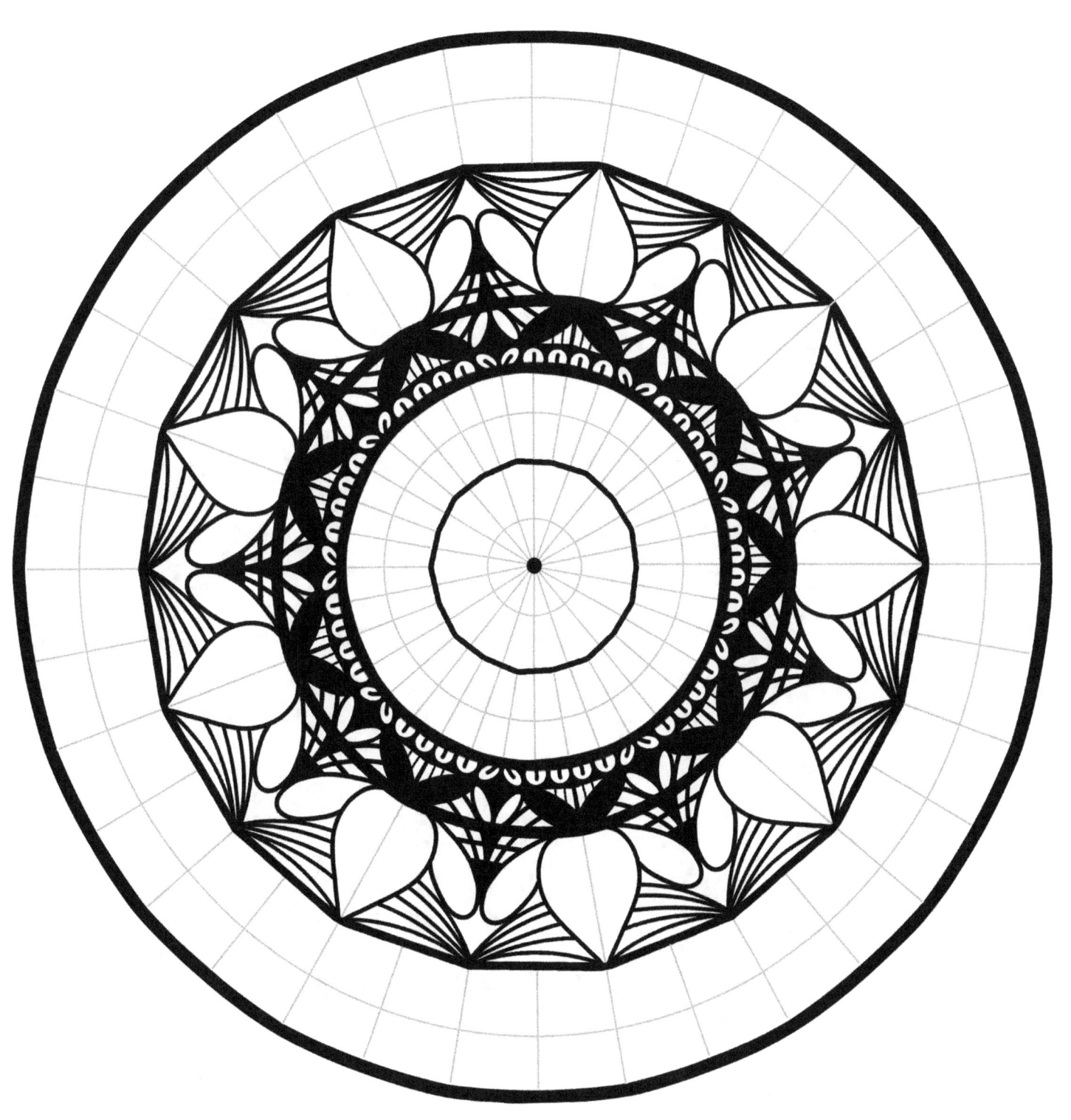

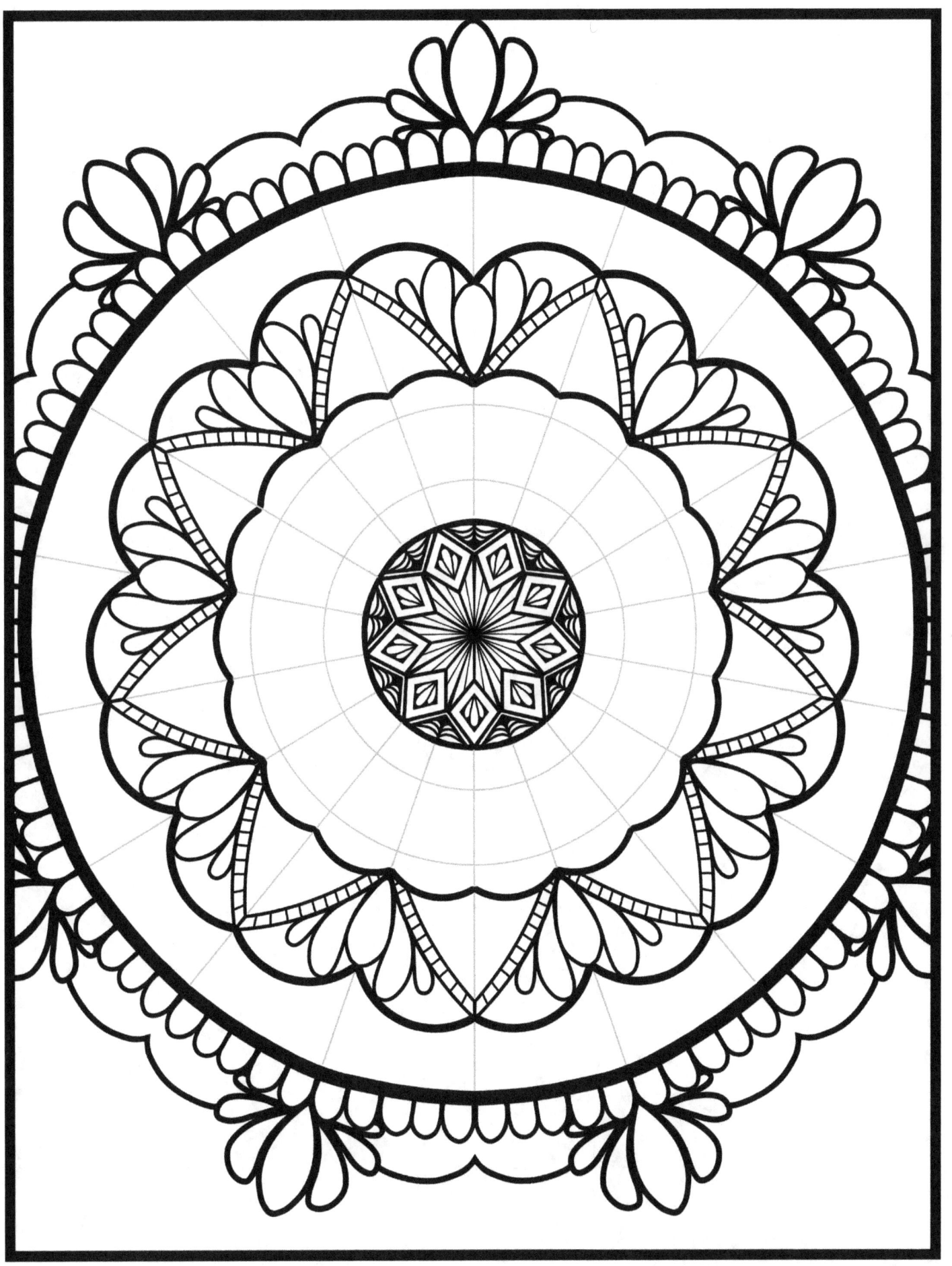

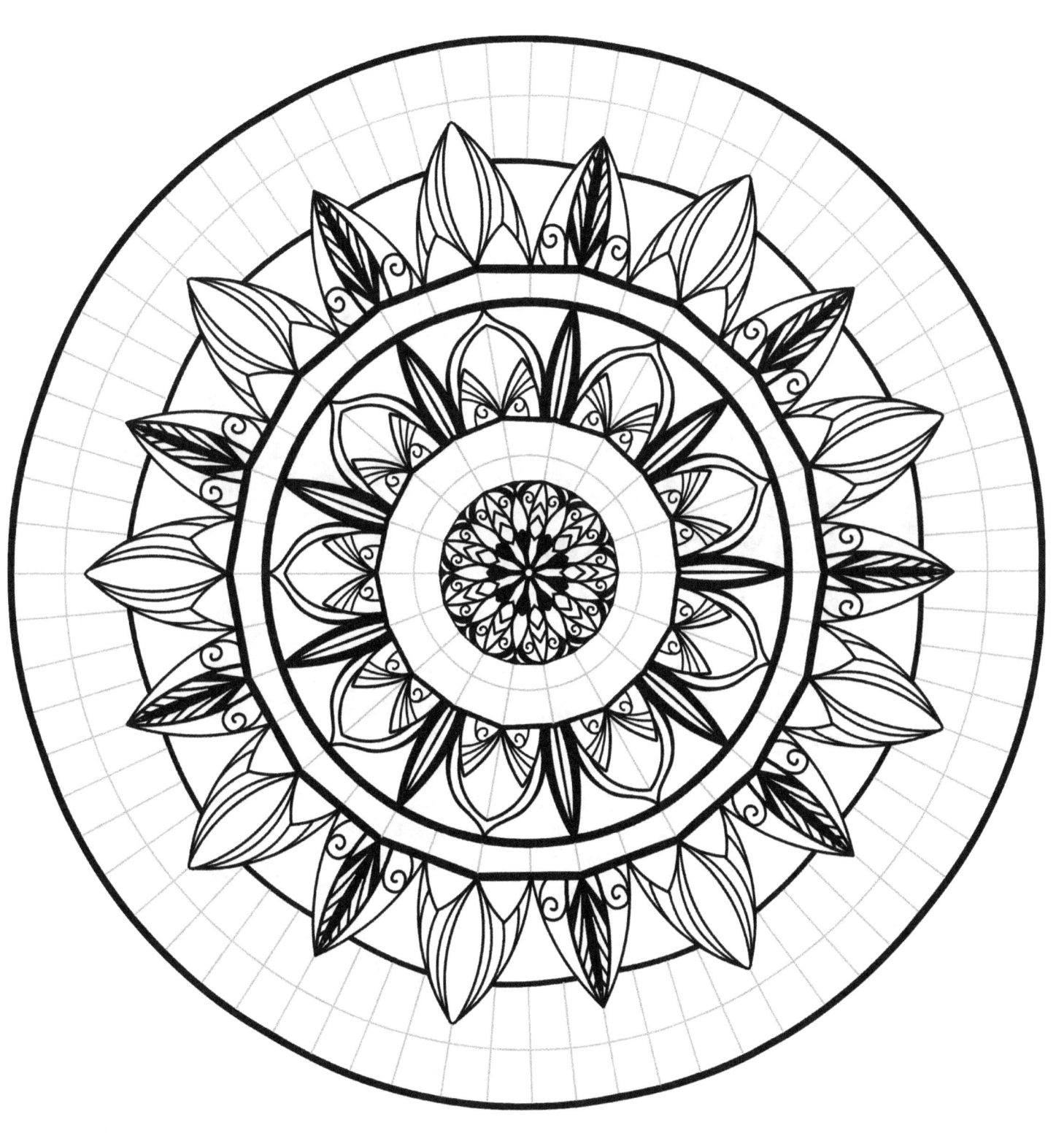

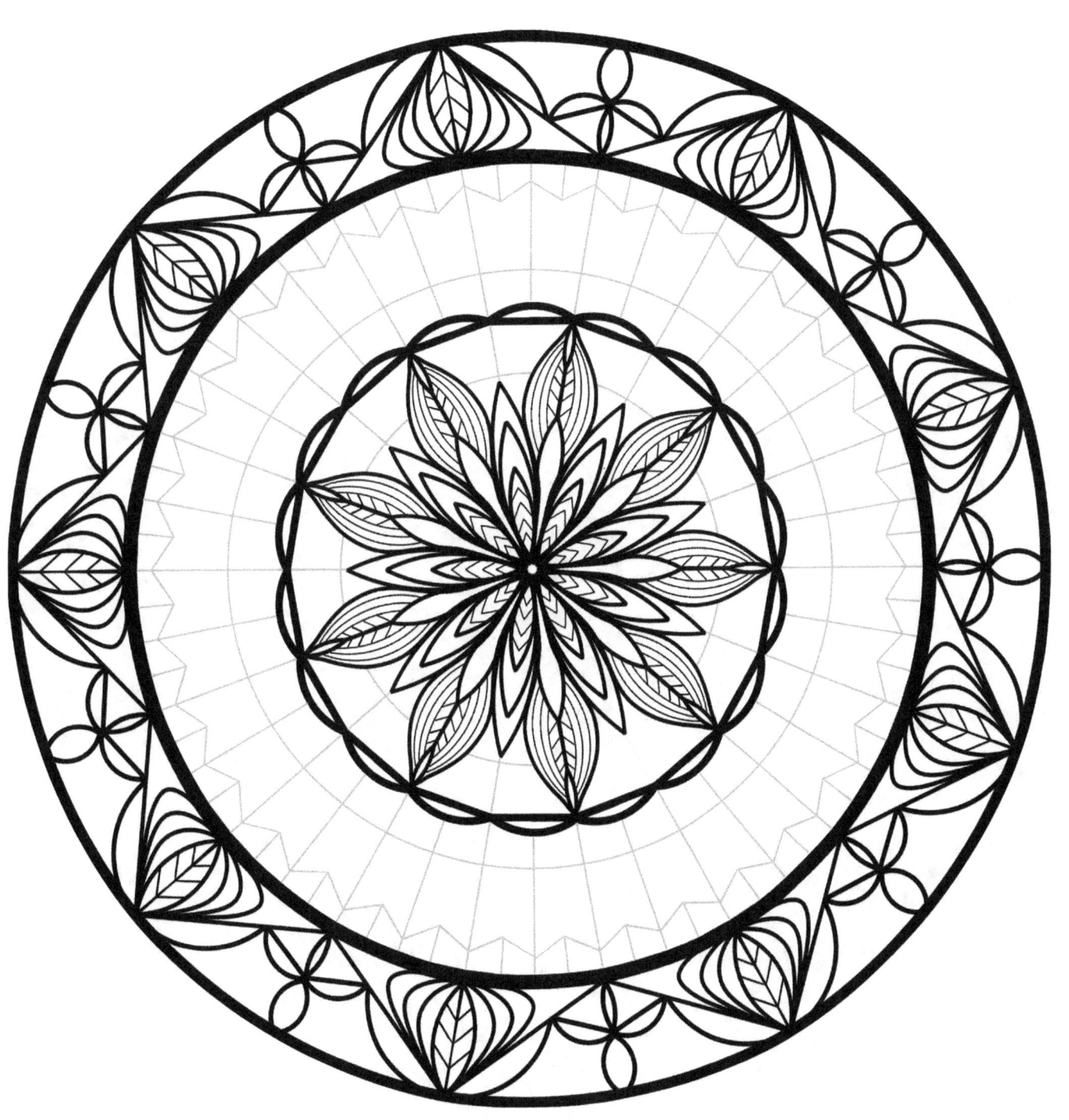

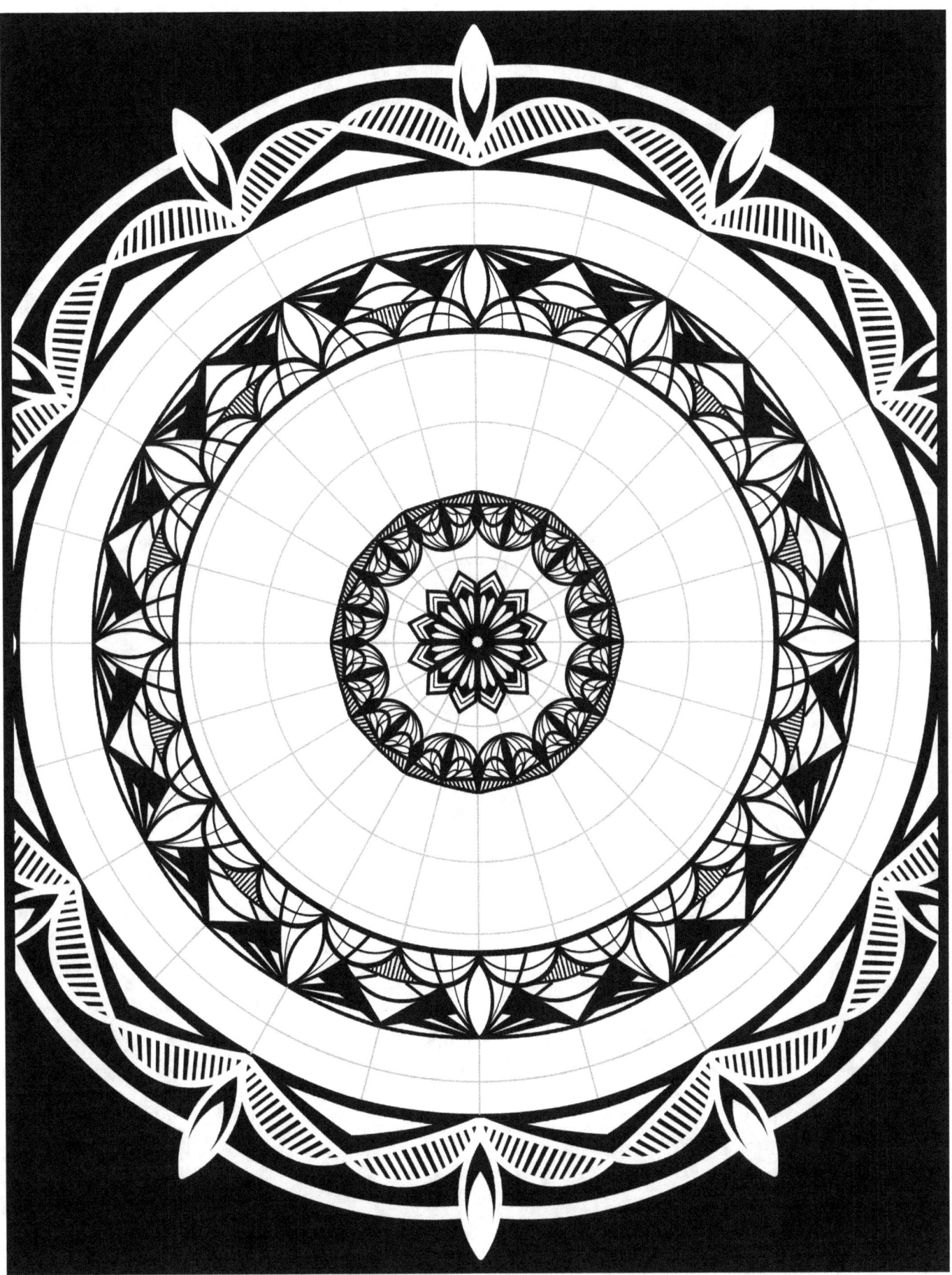

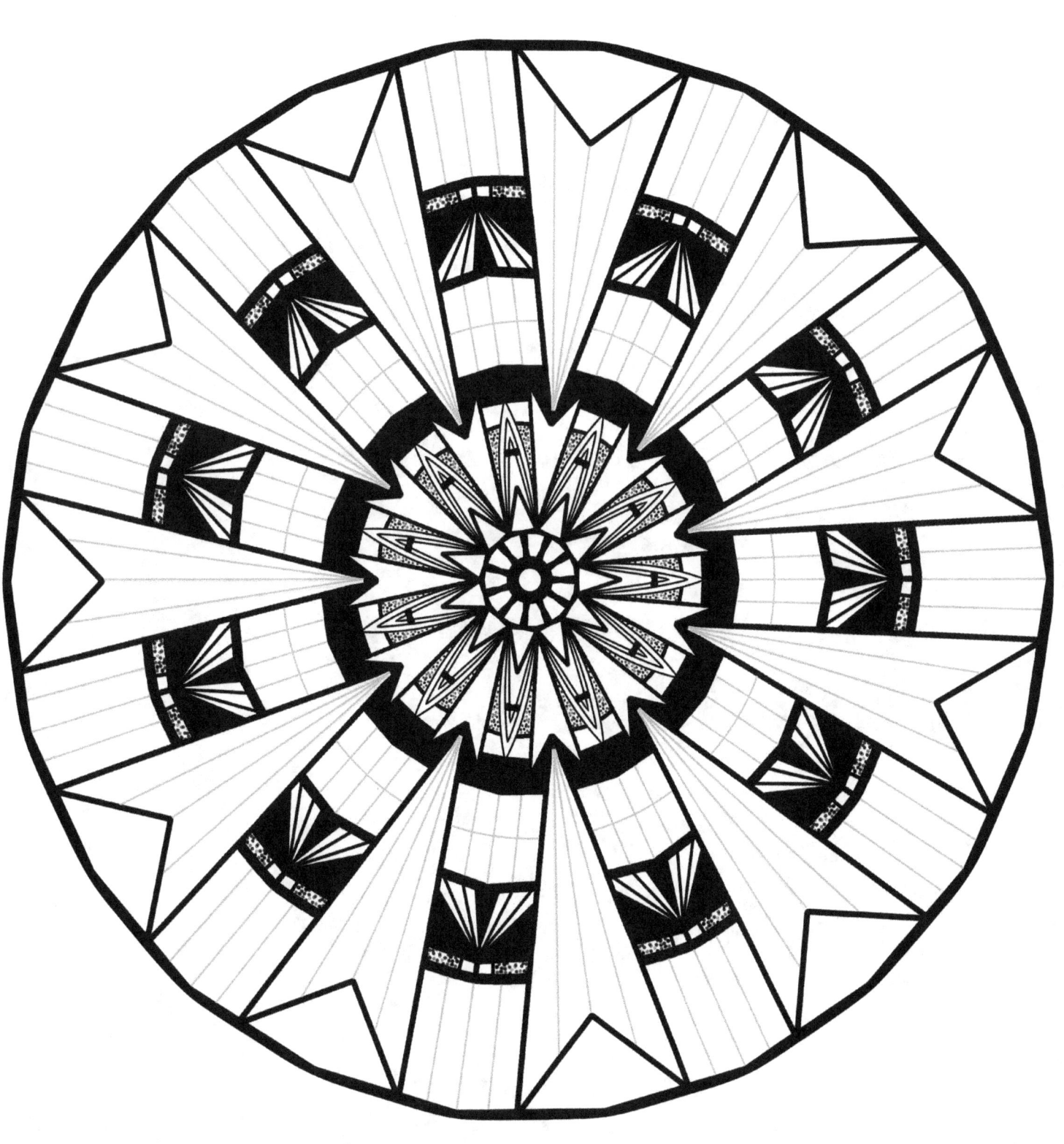

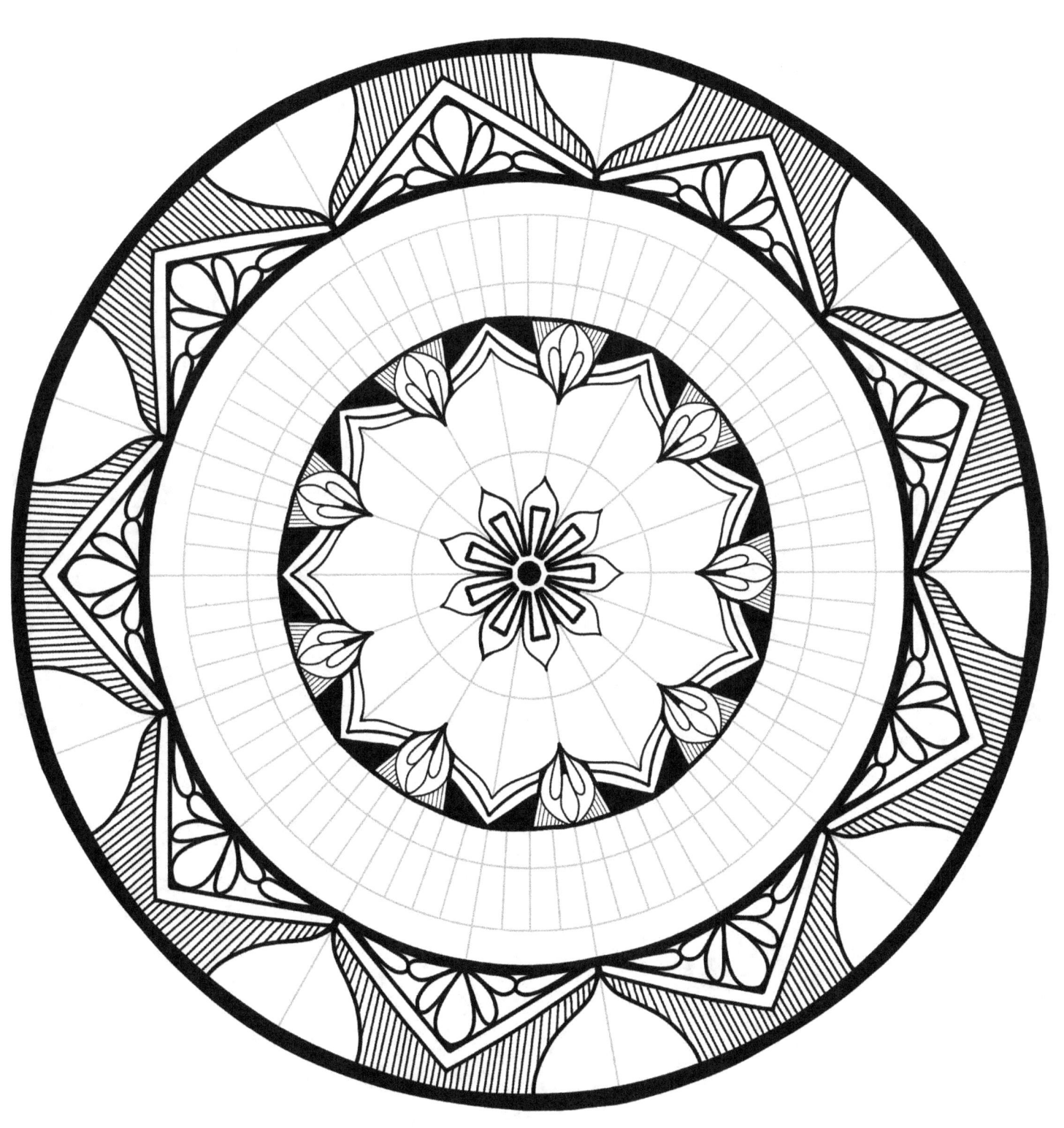

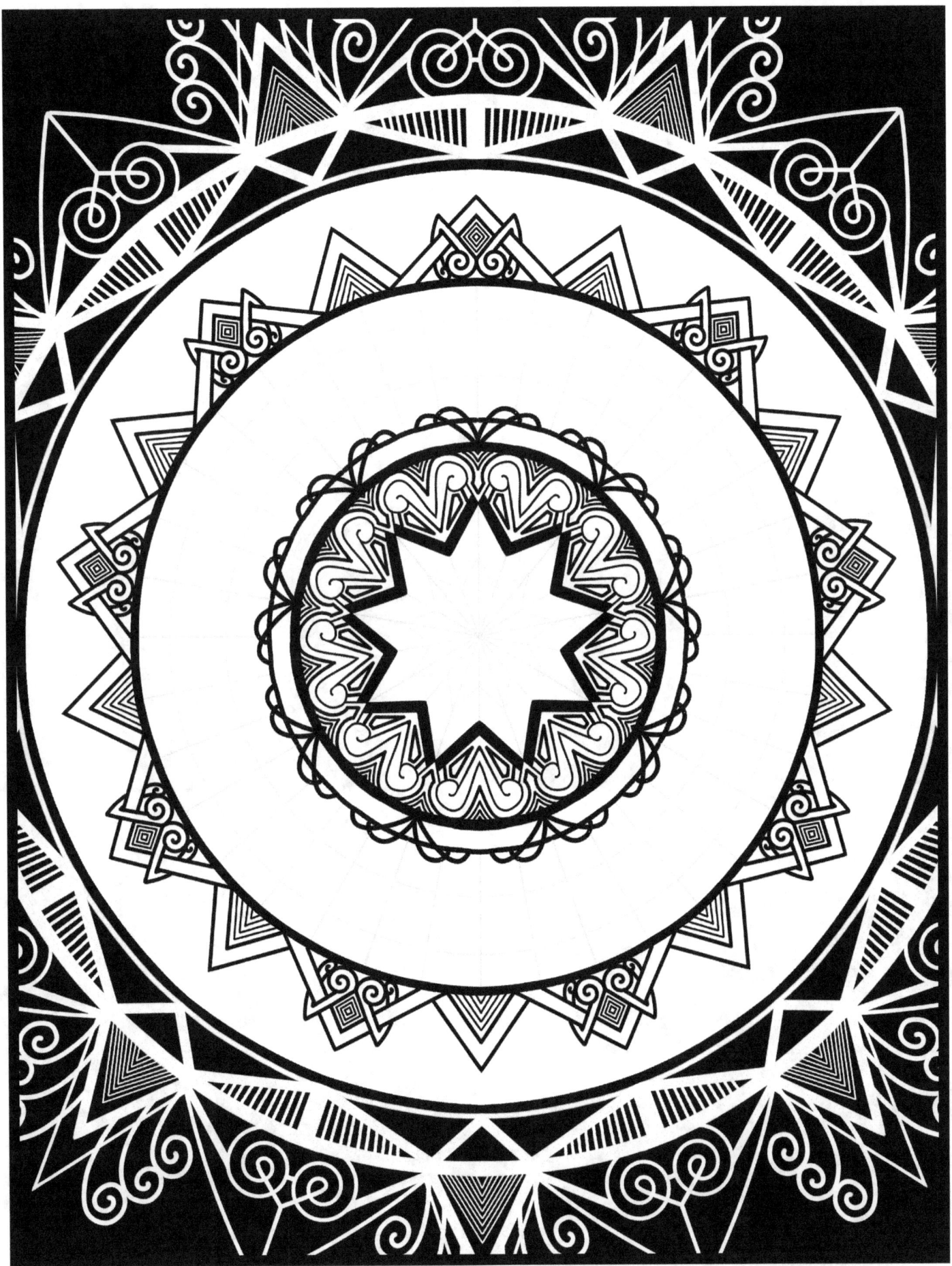

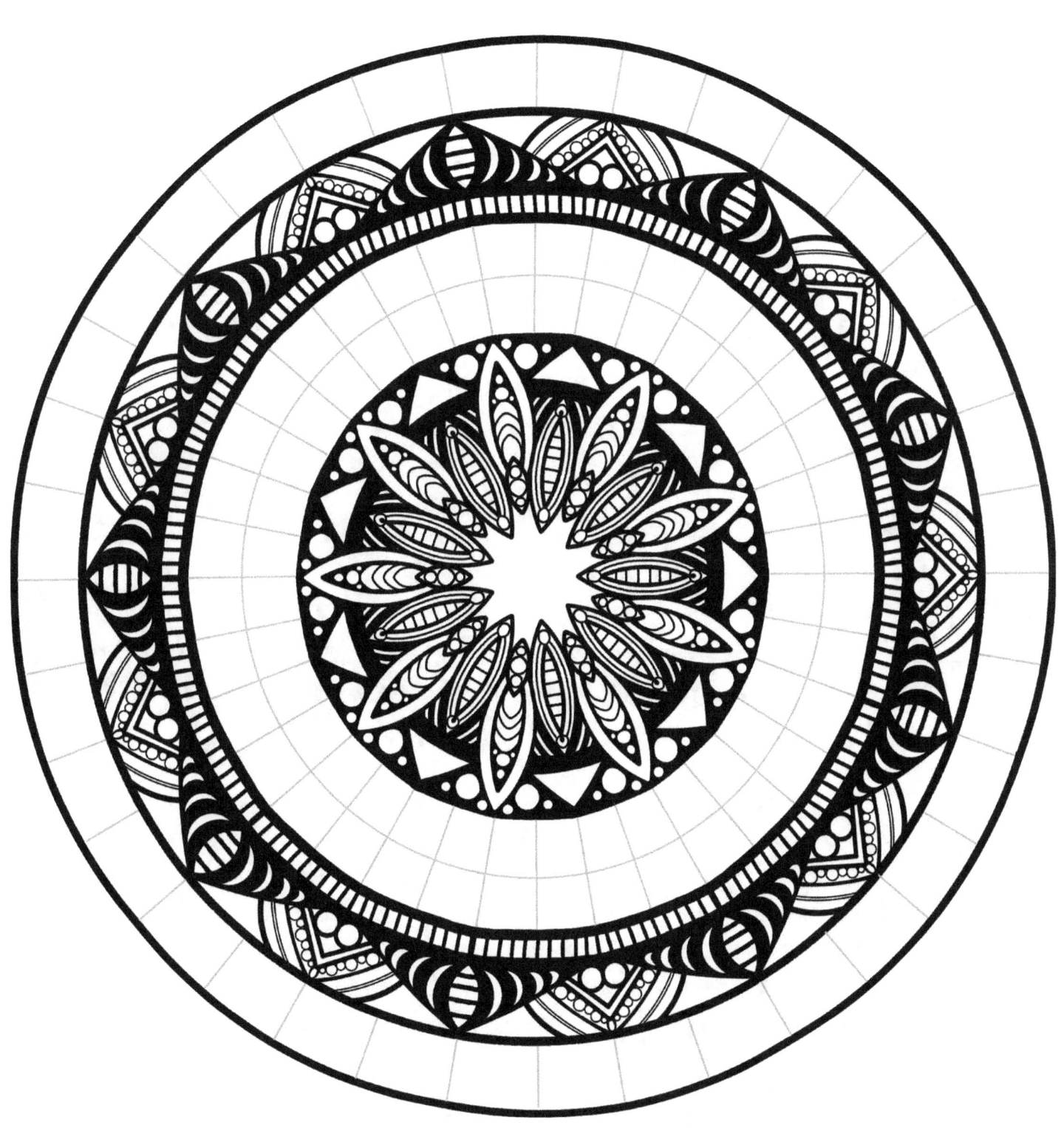

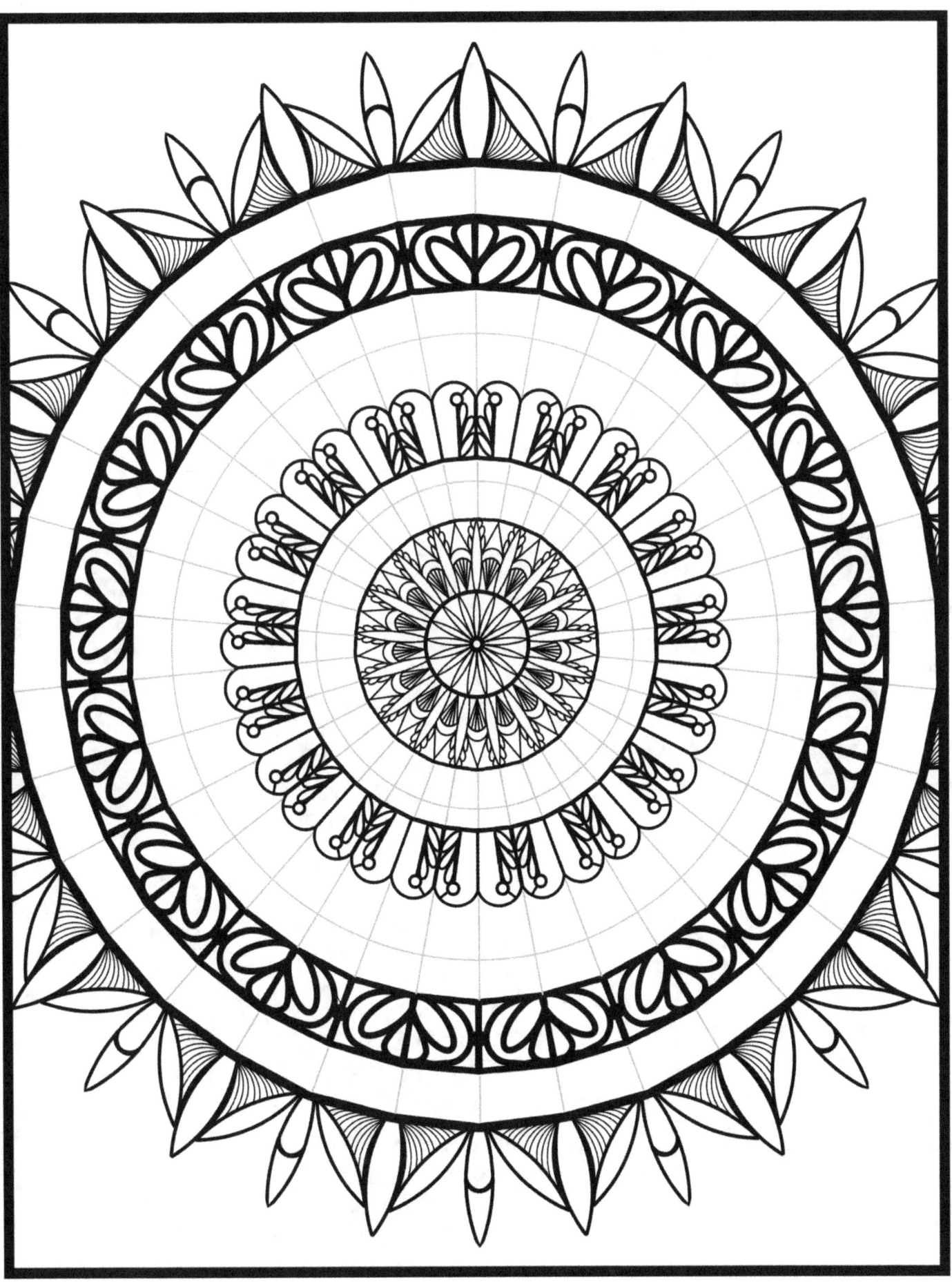

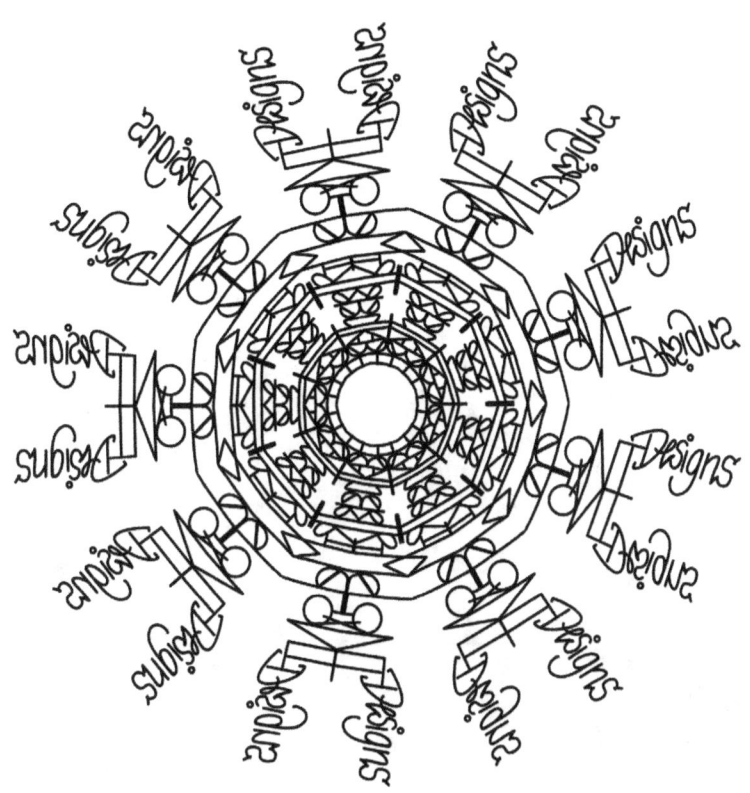

www.ingramcontent.com/pod-product-compliance
Lightning Source LLC
Chambersburg PA
CBHW080536220526
45465CB00015B/2914